D0394572

Mel
Gibson

Titles in the People in the News series include:

Drew Barrymore	Dominique Moceanu
Garth Brooks	Rosie O'Donnell
Jim Carrey	Brad Pitt
Matt Damon	Colin Powell
Princess Diana	Christopher Reeve
Bill Gates	J. K. Rowling
Mel Gibson	The Rolling Stones
John Grisham	Steven Spielberg
Jesse Jackson	R. L. Stine
Michael Jordan	Prince William
Stephen King	Oprah Winfrey
George Lucas	Tiger Woods

PEOPLE
IN THE **NEWS**

Mel Gibson

by Jim McAvoy

Lucent Books, San Diego, CA

No part of this book may be reproduced or used in any form or by any means, electrical, mechanical, or otherwise, including, but not limited to, photocopy, recording, or any information storage and retrieval system, without prior written permission from the publisher.

To my grandmother, Dorothy McAvoy—thanks for encouraging me.

Acknowledgments: Thank you to my parents for their never-ending support; my sister, Connie Cleary; Connie Berman; Bob Harris; Oliver Amudipe; Jarrod Cecere—and to Marla Ryan and Chandra Howard, my editors, for their patience and faith in me.

Library of Congress Cataloging-in-Publication Data

McAvoy, Jim.
  Mel Gibson / by Jim McAvoy.
    p. cm. — (People in the news)
  Includes bibliographical references and index.
  Summary: Discusses the private life and film career of movie star Mel Gibson.
   ISBN 1-56006-980-5 (hardback : alk. paper)
  1. Gibson, Mel—Juvenile literature. 2. Motion picture actors and actresses—Australia—Biography—Juvenile literature. [1. Gibson, Mel. 2. Actors and actresses.] I. Title. II. People in the news (San Diego, Calif.)
  PN3018.G5 M27 2002
  791.43'028'092—dc21

2001003193

Copyright © 2002 by Lucent Books, Inc.
12911 Technology Way, San Diego, CA 92127
Printed in the U.S.A.

Table of Contents

Foreword 6

Introduction
The $25 Million Man 8

Chapter 1
Family First 15

Chapter 2
Getting Serious About Acting 24

Chapter 3
Serious Actor, Serious Pressure 36

Chapter 4
Blockbuster! 47

Chapter 5
Power Player 57

Chapter 6
A New Role 68

Chapter 7
Real-Life Roles 77

Chapter 8
"Millennium Mel" 87

Notes 96
**Important Dates in the Life of
  Mel Gibson** 100
For Further Reading 103
Works Consulted 105
Index 106
Picture Credits 111
About the Author 112

Foreword

FAME AND CELEBRITY are alluring. People are drawn to those who walk in fame's spotlight, whether they are known for great accomplishments or for notorious deeds. The lives of the famous pique public interest and attract attention, perhaps because their experiences seem in some ways so different from, yet in other ways so similar to, our own.

Newspapers, magazines, and television regularly capitalize on this fascination with celebrity by running profiles of famous people. For example, television programs such as *Entertainment Tonight* devote all of their programming to stories about entertainment and entertainers. Magazines such as *People* fill their pages with stories of the private lives of famous people. Even newspapers, newsmagazines, and television news frequently delve into the lives of well-known personalities. Despite the number of articles and programs, few provide more than a superficial glimpse at their subjects.

Lucent's People in the News series offers young readers a deeper look into the lives of today's newsmakers, the influences that have shaped them, and the impact they have had in their fields of endeavor and on other people's lives. The subjects of the series hail from many disciplines and walks of life. They include authors, musicians, athletes, political leaders, entertainers, entrepreneurs, and others who have made a mark on modern life and who, in many cases, will continue to do so for years to come.

These biographies are more than factual chronicles. Each book emphasizes the contributions, accomplishments, or deeds that have brought fame or notoriety to the individual and shows how that person has influenced modern life. Authors portray their subjects in a realistic, unsentimental light. For example, Bill Gates—the cofounder and chief executive officer of the software giant Microsoft—has been instrumental in making personal computers the most vital tool of the modern age. Few dispute his business savvy, his perseverance, or his technical expertise, yet critics say he is ruthless in his dealings with competitors and driven more by his desire to maintain Microsoft's dominance in the computer industry than by an interest in furthering technology.

In these books, young readers will encounter inspiring stories about real people who achieved success despite enormous obstacles. Oprah Winfrey—the most powerful, most watched, and wealthiest woman on television today—spent the first six years of her life in the care of her grandparents while her unwed mother sought work and a better life elsewhere. Her adolescence was colored by promiscuity, pregnancy at age fourteen, rape, and sexual abuse.

Each author documents and supports his or her work with an array of primary and secondary source quotations taken from diaries, letters, speeches, and interviews. All quotes are footnoted to show readers exactly how and where biographers derive their information and provide guidance for further research. The quotations enliven the text by giving readers eyewitness views of the life and accomplishments of each person covered in the People in the News series.

In addition, each book in the series includes photographs, annotated bibliographies, timelines, and comprehensive indexes. For both the casual reader and the student researcher, the People in the News series offers insight into the lives of today's newsmakers—people who shape the way we live, work, and play in the modern age.

The $25 Million Man

BEGINNING IN THE 1990s, paychecks of movie actors, like those of sports figures and other celebrities, soared into the economic stratosphere with rapid speed. Big names like Denzel Washington (for *Courage Under Fire*), Jim Carrey (*The Cable Guy*), Will Smith (*Wild Wild West*), and Leonardo DiCaprio (*The Beach*) demanded and got $10, $15, and even $20 million paychecks for the first time in the history of Hollywood. Actresses also commanded their own hefty salaries. Demi Moore received a reported $12.5 million for the 1996 comedy *Striptease*, and Julia Roberts and Jodie Foster eventually topped Moore with $20 million for *Erin Brockovich* and $15 million for *Anna and the King*, respectively.

Mel Gibson was paid $25 million to star in The Patriot.

As a result of this widespread salary scale overhaul, the entertainment industry eagerly waited to hear the announcement to this paycheck question: Who would become the first star to break the $20 million barrier? By the year 2000 it had the answer: American-born, Australian-bred actor Mel Gibson became the $25 million man, the highest-paid film star in history.

When questioned about his groundbreaking status in the film industry in interviews for *The Patriot*, the film for which he received the hefty amount, Gibson usually changed the subject. Despite his diversionary tactics, the news remained fresh in the minds of journalists and pop culture watchers. Even the *Wall Street Journal* trumpeted the milestone announcement. By the time an entertainment magazine asked the actor about his paycheck while he was making *The Patriot*, he replied, "What am I gonna do, not take it? Look at all the people [the film industry] takes care of—it's kept this town racing. And it keeps a lot of people fed."[1]

Back Story

At the time *The Patriot* was released in late June 2000, Mel Gibson was hardly a newcomer to movies or Hollywood, although his path to stardom may not have been the one most commonly taken. In the late 1970s Gibson had been discovered by a doctor-turned–film director who cast him in a low-budget Australian vigilante picture called *Mad Max*. Soon Gibson became the hottest actor in Australia, a status he cemented in the early 1980s with *Max*'s well-regarded sequel, *The Road Warrior*. *The Road Warrior*'s popularity at the box office and on the still-new medium of videotape brought the actor to the attention of Hollywood casting agents, directors, and the public.

In 1984 Mel Gibson made the first of his Hollywood films. Then, after taking a sixteen-month vacation from movies, Gibson emerged on the screen again in 1987, this time in the guise of a loner cop with a death wish in the buddy cop picture *Lethal Weapon*. With this successful film, the first in a smash-hit series, Gibson's career seemed to have been rejuvenated, and he quickly became one of Hollywood's most sought-after leading men. He followed the first *Weapon* with several subsequent successes and

The violence in The Patriot *was compared to that in* Braveheart (pictured).

his first stab at a Shakespearean role onscreen in Franco Zeffirelli's 1990 adaptation of *Hamlet*–a daunting risk that turned into one of the best decisions of his acting career.

The 1996 thriller *Ransom* found its star in an elite club. For the first time, Mel took home $20 million for the kidnap thriller in an arrangement in which his salary, along with director Ron Howard's and producer Brian Grazer's, came from the film's opening weekend's take. In comparison, Gibson had collected $5 million for *Braveheart* just a year earlier.

In a little over two decades as a working, recognizable film actor, Mel Gibson's films have earned an impressive $1.8 billion, placing him in a league with such superstars as Tom Cruise, Eddie Murphy, and Bruce Willis. And since 1989 he has starred in nine films earning over $100 million at the U.S. box office alone.

The Patriot

The 2000 historical epic *The Patriot* found Gibson back in somewhat familiar territory. The saga of Benjamin Martin–a South Carolina farmer and veteran of the French and Indian War who detests conflict but is forced to fight in America's Revolution—faced the inevitable comparisons to *Braveheart*, the character and the movie. The star found distinctions, however. "What's different with this character is that he's truly afraid of himself, of his own sins. He's always had the feeling there will be retribution for his past misdeeds, which he obviously feels were war crimes."[2]

Gibson was passionate about the story and his character, who was partially based on Revolutionary War figure Francis Marion, nicknamed the "Swamp Fox." He believed so much in the project that he turned down two other blockbusters-to-be, the eventual Best Picture Oscar winner *Gladiator* and *The Perfect Storm*, to make *The Patriot*. Gibson was attracted to the story because "It was a really personal story that put a guy into an extraordinary situation. I love that. . . . There are elements to the story that are shocking, and yet it has to go there to convey the character's desperation."[3]

During the 102 days of filming, beginning in September 1999, Gibson, director Roland Emmerich, and company brought the story of widowed father of seven Benjamin Martin to life on location in the old-fashioned verdancy of Charleston, South Carolina. With a script written by Robert Rodat, who also composed *Saving Private Ryan*, there was plenty of graphic war violence, just as there had been in *Braveheart*.

This included an early sequence in which two of Martin's sons help him kill more than a dozen British soldiers, a potential lightning rod for controversy in a world reeling from real-life violence. But Mel Gibson is not an actor who only takes roles that play it safe. "There was always a revenge story," *Patriot* producer Dean Devlin said during the shoot. "But it began to take on some complexities. It is a genre film, but it transcends that mainly through Mel's willingness to take a character to some very dark places."[4]

Over the more than twenty years he has been in the movie business, Gibson has made a career out of his willingness to take on conflicted characters and risky projects, from *Mad Max* to acting in and directing *Braveheart* and starring in 1999's ultraviolent thriller *Payback*. In fact, he admits that successes in his business are anybody's guess, but that isn't the most important factor he takes into consideration for the parts he chooses. "For me, being comfortable isn't all that interesting,"[5] he has said.

Upon the release of the Revolutionary War epic, *Time* magazine's Richard Schickel wrote,

> We are never unaware of the actor's fundamental good nature, reflected in Martin's fierce, sweet love of family, the casual ease of his action passages. [Gibson] is unquestionably a star who can open a picture. Now we will see if he can, as he did in the even more unlikely *Braveheart*, narrow the distance between the modern audience and far-off history. It is by no means a sure shot. On the other hand, it would be almost unpatriotic to bet against him.[6]

Entertainment Weekly put its own spin on Gibson's capabilities when describing Martin's confrontation with his bitter enemy, Colonel Tavington, in the second half of the nearly three-hour film. Promising to avenge his loved one's death by killing Tavington, Gibson could have been caught off guard when the filmmakers and the actor playing Tavington, Jason Isaacs, decided to improvise without his knowledge. "Why wait?" Isaac's dastardly redcoat ad-libbed to the grief-stricken Martin. And Gibson's Martin retorted with a controlled, one-word, soft-spoken response: "Soon."

"One reason studios don't flinch at paying Gibson $25 million, the richest fee of any actor, is such inventiveness," the magazine declared. "Adding a glimmer of madness, as he's consistently done with his portrayal of Los Angeles detective Martin Riggs in the *Lethal Weapon* series, has only drawn audiences closer to him."[7] On another occasion, the magazine noted that Gibson is one of the few actors who can typically be counted on to promote his projects (after a brief period of press shyness during the mid-'80s).

Expectations for 2000's *The Patriot* were high for Gibson and the movie's studio, Columbia TriStar. In fact, the film's opening was pitted against *The Perfect Storm*, which Gibson had turned down, over the lucrative July 4 holiday weekend in 2000. But *The Perfect Storm* won the holiday weekend's box-office showdown with $42 million, $20 million more than *The Patriot*'s earnings during that period of time.

Although the Revolutionary War epic earned $113 million in the United States and an additional $102 million overseas, making it the seventeenth highest-grossing movie of 2000, it was not the blockbuster many assumed it would be, and talk of nominations and awards turned out to be just that—mostly talk. (Gibson did win two People's Choice Awards: Motion Picture Star in a Drama for *The Patriot* and the general Motion Picture Actor trophy.) Still, Gibson remains proud of *The Patriot*, recently calling it "a really superior film."[8] But Gibson has admitted that choosing a potentially successful film over a box-office flop is not an exact science—for him or for anyone else. "[It's] always a crapshoot. Nobody knows anything, and I include myself in the multitude of the ignorant. There's no gauge. I've seen great films, perfect almost, that never do any business. Something didn't make everyone go. And I've seen real pieces of garbage work

Famous Relative

Mel Gibson in not the only famous member of his family—or the only talented one. His paternal grandmother, Eva Mylott, was a well-known opera singer on two continents, Australia and North America.

Mylott left her native Australia at the beginning of the twentieth century to sing in America, just as her grandson would one day leave his Australian home to seek fame and fortune abroad. She made her home in the Midwest, where she married John Hutton Gibson, and become a popular contralto on opera stages in Chicago and in parts of Canada. She gave birth to Mel's father, Hutton Peter Gibson, in 1918. Still a young woman, she died in 1920, after her second son, Alexander Mylott, was born.

Today her family home and birthplace, Tuross Head, off the southern coast of New South Wales, is a popular vacation resort and tourist attraction.

like gangbusters. . . . You can make an educated guess, but after that it's a crapshoot."[9]

Guessing game or not, audiences regularly cheer Gibson's onscreen heroics and routinely spend their hard-earned cash to see his latest motion picture. But it took him years to get to where he is now—a top movie star, director, and producer. Once criticized for his "tendency to stand around looking internationally handsome,"[10] Mel Gibson has come a long way from his humble beginnings.

Chapter 1

Family First

FAMILY HAS always played a major role in grounding Mel Gibson's life. His parents, Hutton (called "Hutt" or "Red" for the color of his hair) and Anna (also called Ann) Gibson, married in May 1944, and told everyone they wanted to have 10 children. In time, they made good on their promise, with their first child arriving about a year after they were married.

Debut

The sixth of their brood, Mel Columcille Gerard Gibson, was born on January 3, 1956, in Peekskill, New York, about thirty-nine miles north of New York City. At the time the family was living in Verplanck's Point, a largely Irish and Italian community four miles south of Peekskill on the eastern bank of the Hudson River. Columcille (pronounced "Colum-kill") honors both the town in Ireland where Anna Gibson was born and an ancient Irish saint, while Gerard is for Saint Gerard Majella, the patron saint of expectant mothers in the Roman Catholic faith. Anna and Hutt Gibson were religious people, and Anna would pray to Saint Gerard each time she was pregnant to ensure a safe delivery. Mel followed elder siblings Patricia, Sheila, Mary Bridget, Kevin, and Maura and in time was big brother to identical twins Danny and Chris, followed by Donal, and, lastly, Ann.

While residing in Verplanck's Point, the family lived in a modest home with several bedrooms, an attic, and a small yard. When Hutt Gibson, a New York Central Railroad brakeman, and Anna, a homemaker, moved into the house in Verplanck's Point, they had three children. When they moved out several years later, they were parents to nine. Soon after, their tenth child was born.

Gibson was born in Peekskill, New York (pictured in this historical photo), and has several brothers and sisters.

In later years Mel Gibson reflected fondly on his upbringing.

> My parents were religious working-class people who at the same time were very well-educated—particularly my father—in literature, languages, and philosophy. Philosophical and theological discussions [and] canon law were a part of our upbringing. My parents were smart people and they chose not to live in opulence. They shared all they had with a large family, and it was a loving one.[11]

Both parents, but especially Hutt Gibson, ran a strict, religious household. A longtime friend of the family, also a brakeman, recalled, "A lot of people used to let their kids just run off, but [Hutt] never did. . . . He had close contact with them from the time they got up in the morning until nighttime; he knew where they were."[12]

The Gibson children were very well behaved, which is attributed to their parents' good example. The friend continued that the kids

> never got in trouble. They were a close-knit family. . . . The family was outstanding. I don't think there's anybody who could say that they disliked them. And not a bad word would ever come out of Red. . . . A curse word? You never heard it. If something ever happened to somebody, the first thing he'd be saying was prayers. And [Anna], too, was a very nice, very pleasant woman.[13]

Farm Life

As part of his American dream for his growing family, it had been Hutt Gibson's wish to raise his growing family on land of their own. When Mel was five, the brood moved to a farm in Mount Vision, New York, a bit farther north than Verplanck's Point. With their move came the chance to cultivate their own land and grow their own provisions, something that appealed to the ever-increasing clan.

While luxuries were few for the Gibson family, Hutt Gibson worked hard to provide for his wife and children. During the time they lived in Mount Vision, he was promoted at the railroad, which was quite a distance from the farm. Most nights during the week he would stay in Brooklyn, where Anna's parents lived, and he'd spend the weekend back on the farm with the rest of his family. "None of us could complain," Gibson has said. "Even with all those brothers and sisters, we each got tons of attention growing up. We attended to one another, and my parents never even went out to dinner—they were always there for us."[14]

While Gibson's recollections may sound happy, there were setbacks during the time the Gibsons lived in Mount Vision. With little growing experience or knowledge of the land, successful farming did not come as naturally as they had hoped. A spring above their farmhouse froze, cutting off their water supply one winter. Plus, the growing season was short because of the frigid upstate New York winter temperatures.

Mischievous Youngster

Mel Gibson is fondly remembered as a child. A former Verplanck's Point neighbor, Margaret Smith Saladino, once recalled Mel's natural likability as a youngster. "When I was sixteen I was Mel's first baby-sitter. . . . I think Mel was always my favorite [of the Gibson children]. I don't know why. Probably it was because of his personality. He was kind of a happy-go-lucky kid. All smiles. . . . He may have been kind of a little devil, but he was the sort who could get away with it because he was so cute."

Mel was a mischievous tyke. For example, he and his brothers held roof-jumping contests from their barn when they lived in Mount Vision. Although young Mel did occasionally misbehave, such as when he stapled one of his sisters' heads, he was not normally a problem child. "I wasn't a holy terror—it was more passive-aggressive," he admits.

He also enjoyed entertaining by telling jokes to family members. The Gibson brothers enjoyed watching The Three Stooges and Humphrey Bogart movies on TV to pass the time, and Mel considered the rugged actor one of his heroes. His other hero? His dad, Hutton.

The hardest time of all came in December 1964, when Hutt Gibson was injured while working aboard a train engine. He had slipped on some oil and fallen onto the tracks and the underlying roadbed. As a result, he suffered severe injuries to his back and spine, and several serious, painful operations were required to undo the damage. The family prayed and looked to other means for financial survival.

Hard Times Ahead

With Hutt Gibson out of work and waging what was to be a long legal war against his former employer, the Mount Vision property had to be sold. The family then moved into a large home in a mountainous town called Salisbury Mills, New York, directly across the Hudson River from their old neighborhood, Verplanck's Point. Two of Mel's older sisters went to work to help support the family during these financially tough days. One was employed as an assistant to a librarian, while the other took a position at a newspaper.

With his children helping out, there was a unique way for Hutt to make money and keep the large brood afloat. He was by all accounts a well-educated man, and he turned a successful stint on the television game show *Jeopardy!* into a small fortune for that time–approximately $21,000. "If it wasn't for the quiz shows," Anna Gibson's older sister Kathleen once admitted to a journalist, "they wouldn't have had anything."[15]

Pleased with his quiz-show winnings but worried about his family's future, Hutt investigated new career opportunities. It was obvious that he wouldn't be working at the railroad again, especially with his court case still pending; the trial had been pushed back several times. After taking aptitude test after aptitude test, Hutt Gibson was notified that he possessed a genius IQ. With that declaration, it was suggested that he try the burgeoning field of computer programming. After another back operation, he enrolled in courses in New York City and soon began a long career as a computer programmer.

In February 1968, more than three years after his accident on the railroad, Hutt Gibson's case against the New York Central Railroad finally went to court in White Plains, New York. Although Hutt had originally sued for $250,000, a motion for the amount of $2 million was filed by Hutt's lawyer due to a complication of his injury but was denied by the court. After a week, however, Hutt Gibson tasted victory as the jury awarded him $145,000 on Valentine's Day of that year. The family's long struggle with near poverty had come to an end.

An International Move

After the upheaval of the last few years and now in a financially secure position, in the summer of 1968 Hutt and Anna Gibson made an important decision that surprised just about everyone. The escalating Vietnam War was creating widespread protest in the United States. Like so many others, the Gibsons opposed the conflict, and they decided to move the family to Sydney, Australia, halfway around the world. Years later Mel Gibson would address this reason for the move: "My older brother was about to get drafted and my father didn't want to send his sons out to get jungle rot or worse. He didn't want to send us off one by one to get chopped up."[16]

There were other reasons for the international relocation as well. Mel's parents were acutely aware that the America of the late 1960s, with its rampant drug use and sexual promiscuity, was vastly different from the one they wanted their children to grow up in. They felt the children could have a more moral-centered rearing in an old-fashioned place like Australia. Besides, Hutt Gibson's mother had been born there, so it was a return to his roots.

In later years Mel Gibson downplayed the Vietnam War as a cause for the move, saying his parents—especially his father, Hutt—just desired a change. Whatever the case, after attending a good-bye party in Brooklyn thrown in their honor by Anna Gibson's sister Kathleen, the Gibsons were off on their trip in July 1968. But the Gibsons didn't go straight to their new home country. Instead, Anna and Hutt thought it should be an enlightening, educational trip for their many school-aged children. They toured Ireland (still home to some of Anna's relatives at the time), England, and Italy. Patricia Gibson, who had joined a convent, and Kevin Gibson, a seminary student, also traveled

Gibson's parents moved their family to Sydney, Australia, partly because they opposed the fighting in Vietnam and wanted to protect their children.

The Gibsons traveled to three countries in Europe before settling in Sydney (pictured).

with the rest of the clan, after being released from their respective religious orders.

A few months later the family arrived in Melbourne in Victoria, Australia. They quickly settled into their new home in suburban Sydney, the capital of New South Wales. A local newspaper, the *Melbourne Herald*, even ran a story about the Gibsons when they arrived, playing up the size of the large brood. The family had been met by a press photographer at the airport who thought their move was newsworthy, and they agreed to sit for a photo and an interview. And keeping good on a promise to God, should they arrive safely in their new country, the family gained a member when Anna and Hutt adopted an infant, Andrew, shortly after arriving Down Under.

School Days

Settling into their new life after the move, Hutt and Anna Gibson sent Mel to Saint Leo's College, an all-boys Catholic school run by the Christian Brothers, a strict religious order. Friends were hard to come by at first for the transplanted "Yank," which is what his Australian classmates nicknamed the shy, skinny youth with the intense blue eyes. "I had a fairly rough time of it," he remembered years later about his Catholic school days in his new country. "It was all right. [The Christian Brothers] had a hard-line

Gibson liked to participate in sports but was not very good at surfing.

discipline, which ain't all bad. When I was there I really rebelled against it, but you've got to toe the line sometime."[17]

The move to Australia had come at an especially sensitive time for preteen Mel. "I was the tender age of 12—on the eve of puberty—which is upheaval time anyway," Gibson has commented. "To actually switch cultures . . . there was excitement and adventure but also trepidation. I remember those conflicting feelings very clearly."[18] As he grew into his teenage years, Mel began to rebel. At times the strict upbringing at home and school brought out the worst in him, and his grades suffered. Not surprisingly, he had developed an interest in dating girls, and he had taken up smoking cigarettes and drinking. Needless to say, Mel's strict parents did not approve.

Hutt Gibson was not satisfied with the education his son was receiving at Saint Leo's. After attending the school for a year, Mel was transferred to Asquith High School, a state-run educational institution, at his father's request. There his grades improved somewhat, and he made friends more easily with his Australian classmates. In addition to trying everything from rugby to basketball to soccer, young Mel also attempted surfing, Australia's unofficial national sport, but he admits he wasn't very good at it.

Although happier and improving scholastically after his transfer to Asquith High, Mel still did not particularly excel in his studies there. As high school wound down, he had to put more thought into life after graduation. He had already decided against religious life, after briefly considering entering the priesthood, and he also entertained a brief dream of becoming a journalist. He made the decision not to attend college. Without much effort, he landed a job at an orange juice factory, but he was not very pleased with his new job.

Turning Point

During that summer everything changed for eighteen-year-old Gibson. His family could see that working in the juice factory was not satisfying him and perhaps he would be better off elsewhere. His older sister Mary, a onetime drama student at Syracuse University, had watched his amusing antics since he was a little boy, and she could see that her brother had grown into a handsome, athletic young man. Without telling him, his sister sent an application in Gibson's name, his photo, and a $5 registration fee to Australia's renowned National Institute of Dramatic Art (NIDA) at the University of New South Wales. Weeks later a letter from the school arrived for Gibson, including a date for an audition.

He was shocked at what his sister had done. But after some consideration, he thought, "Well, why not? Why not two days out of my life?" He figured the audition couldn't be worse than his job at the juice factory. Later Gibson admitted that he was sure he "was going to make a jerk of myself in front of a lot of people."[19]

The audition was not the embarrassing ordeal Mel had assumed it would be. "They made us do all these silly things," he has recalled. "Improvise, sing, dance. I know I was terrible, but it seemed good then. I guess they saw something raw in me. The guy asked me why I wanted to be an actor and I said, 'I've been goofing around all my life. I thought I might as well get paid for that.' And I got in."[20] The Gibsons' path from upstate New York to Sydney, Australia, had unexpectedly led young Mel to acting and the stage, courtesy of his sister Mary. But it was up to Gibson alone to prove that he belonged there.

Chapter 2

Getting Serious About Acting

AFTER QUITTING his job at the juice factory in 1974, Gibson began attending classes at the NIDA at the University of New South Wales. At first he wasn't sure he belonged there, and others shared this view. His fellow students took their acting studies very seriously, while Gibson was more interested in goofing off than learning the nuances of the craft. At best, he hoped to find a job with a local theater company. Over time, however, his attitude toward acting changed, and his career started solidly in 1979.

Acting Lessons

In the mid-'80s Gibson spoke about his early NIDA days while explaining his attraction to the acting profession. "I remember they would sit us all down and ask us, 'Why do you want to become an actor?'" he remembered.

> They asked everyone and everyone had an answer. And I was scared to death because I, honestly, didn't. I did not know. So the guy asked me and I just turned red and closed up. He sort of had to prod me. "Is it because you enjoy or like doing it?" he asked, and I said, "Oh yeah, sure." And he said, "Okay, that's good enough." And it is good enough. That's the best answer I can give, even today. I enjoy doing it. I like doing it.[21]

But that was not entirely the case when he began taking acting classes in 1974. Years later, when asked if he liked acting right away, Gibson admitted, "No, I didn't. But I found it something I couldn't let go of quite, because it had me by the . . . the things they bat around at Wimbledon. You know? It kind of teased me. It was frustrating."[22]

Gibson's aversion to taking the craft seriously became frustrating for his teachers and fellow NIDA students, too. Many of Gibson's classmates, who included future well-known actors Judy Davis and Geoffrey Rush, were Method actors, who got into their characters by "becoming" them, even acting their parts when the exercise, play, or show was over. Gibson did not share this intense philosophy. Once he was almost thrown out of a class because he refused to perform an acting exercise he thought was a waste of time. Of course, he had thought about being an actor as a child, much the way one fleetingly aspires to be a fireman or a ballerina. But it was only after he began attending NIDA that he gave some real thought—and effort—to the profession.

In 1977, Gibson (right) and Geoffrey Rush starred in Waiting for Godot *at the National Institute of Dramatic Art in New South Wales.*

As his schooling continued, Gibson began to make a real effort and took acting more seriously as he learned to appreciate the craft and the creative doors it opened for him. His efforts soon blossomed, and he found himself with a reputation as a scene stealer in school productions of *Romeo and Juliet* and other plays. "You could never really give him a small part, because he'd take over the play," his movement coach at NIDA, Keith Bain, has said. "He was once given a very small role as a very dumb soldier. When I look back on that production, it is Mel's performance that I remember more than any other."[23]

An interesting development occurred during this time regarding Gibson's appearance. Showbiz legend has it that Gibson's good looks remained somewhat undetected at this time. It was only when he cut his 1970s-era shoulder-length hair for a play set in the 1940s that his true appearance was revealed, leading fans the world over and future costars like Sigourney Weaver and Julia Roberts to swoon over him.

After his second year at the school, Gibson exercised some newfound independence, which he had developed at NIDA. He moved out of his parents' home and in with three friends. Though they took their acting seriously, they also found time to chase after women and throw the occasional out-of-control party.

Screen Debut

While still in school in 1976, Gibson and his friend and classmate Steve Bisley were approached to appear in a film called *Summer City* by a writer/producer named Phil Avalon, also one of the movie's stars. Originally, an actor named Nick Papadopoulous was set to play the role of the surfer Scollop, but personal problems forced him out of the project. Another actor in the film, John Jarratt, suggested that Avalon try actor-in-training Mel Gibson.

Most American film lovers have never heard of this film, in which Gibson sported blond hair. There's a good reason for that: It was never released theatrically anywhere but in Australia, much to Gibson's relief. (It *was* released on video in the United States several years later under the titles *Summer City* and *Coast of Terror* to capitalize on Mel's newfound stardom.)

Gibson clearly has little affection for the film, a mishmash of several genres with only a loose plot surrounding surfing, sex, and violence. "It was an abomination, a cheap, nasty flick that was cranked out in three weeks on a budget of $20,000, and was all about a bunch of young guys out for a good time. My character was a nineteen-year-old surfer who simply surfed and acted dumb, which was all I could possibly handle at the time."[24] Gibson and his costars were paid just $400, the actors' union minimum, for their work in the film and pitched in around the set when it was needed. After shooting was completed, he returned to his studies at NIDA and graduated in the fall of 1977. *Summer City* had only a fair reception at the box office.

Another reason Gibson might not fondly remember *Summer City* has to do with a more personal situation. During filming he was briefly involved with one of the actresses in the film, Debbie Forman. After Gibson broke up with her, Forman slashed her wrists at a party that he also attended. Gibson rushed to Forman's aid at the time, but she fought off his help. Fortunately, she survived, but Gibson was quite troubled by Forman's actions. Forman and Gibson spoke only one time later, several months afterward, when he encouraged Forman to audition for a play she was considering.

While Gibson's good looks had impressed some who had seen *Summer City*—Phil Avalon and the director, Christopher Fraser, even wrote extra scenes for him after watching early footage from the film—it remained to be seen if he was more than just a handsome face onscreen.

Becoming a Professional Actor

Bill Shanahan, one of Australia's most powerful agents at the time, noticed Gibson's performance, and they began a business relationship that netted Gibson a stint on the popular soap opera *The Sullivans* and roles in the TV shows *Punishment* and *The Hero*. But the actor took an instant dislike to TV, with its emphasis on quickly producing the shows rather than spending time on character development or detail. For many years afterward, Gibson stayed away from the medium of television, outside of awards show appearances, some occasional voice-over work, and a hosting stint on *Saturday Night Live* in 1988.

Max

The night of his graduation from acting school, Gibson's attractive face would take a beating. Gibson recalled that night eight years later in an interview.

> I was in this bar, minding my own business, when these three drunks, big guys, decided to make mincemeat out of me. And they did. Don't ask me why, I never found out. Maybe they didn't like my face, which they proceeded to rearrange. Even though I was in pretty good shape, I was no match for all of them. And just like one of the fake fights, this one started in the bar and wound up outside on the street. God, they were all over me. They hit me in the face so many times I couldn't see. They blackened my eyes, flattened my nose, kicked me around like a soccer ball, and left my face like a busted grapefruit.[25]

Gibson spent the remainder of that night in 1977 in the hospital, where he endured unimaginable pain. To add pressure to the situation, he was supposed to accompany an actor friend to an important film audition the next day.

He was somewhat relieved upon arriving for the audition to learn that the filmmakers, including George Miller, a physician–turned–rookie director, were seeking some rough-looking people, since the movie, called *Mad Max*, took place in the post-apocalyptic future. Surprisingly, the brawl at the bar the night before turned out to be a blessing in disguise, since Gibson could now try out for the film—his appearance could perfectly fit what the filmmakers desired—and almost certainly be in the running for a bit role if nothing else.

Although Gibson hadn't really intended to audition himself, he did. Believing he was trying for a supporting role, within a couple of weeks he was awarded that of the title character, "Mad" Max Rockatansky, a cop whose wife and child are killed by gang leaders and who only wants revenge. The vast amount of the script depends on the latter part, with much violence and bloodshed ensuing. Released in 1979 in Australia and 1980 in the United States, Gibson later said of the film: "*Mad Max* was scary as hell. I didn't know what was going on. That film would

Internet Hoax

In 2000 a widely circulated story appeared on the Internet that might have grown out of the true barroom incident the night before Gibson's *Mad Max* audition, proving his iconic place in American cinema. The story is credited to radio personality Paul Harvey, who, when questioned about responsibility for the story responded, "A distorted story about Mel Gibson is being credited to my radio broadcast. Don't believe everything on the Internet."

The story told of a handsome young American man who had moved to Australia with his family. The youth, who entertained dreams of becoming an actor or circus trapeze artist, worked in a bad part of town. While walking home one night, he was beaten by five robbers, who kicked him with their boots and hit him with clubs, leaving him bloodied, his face a mass of wounds, and clinging to life. When the police arrived, he was so banged up that they thought he was dead and called for a car from the morgue.

While on the way to the morgue, a policeman heard the young man gasp for air and took him to the emergency room instead, where the attending nurse remarked with horror that he no longer had a face.

The young man survived the night but spent a long recovery period in the hospital. Upon release, everything but his face had healed—he was no longer an attractive young man. Interviewing for a job, he was repeatedly turned down because of his disfigurement. Someone even cruelly suggested he join a freak show as the "Man with No Face." He took the advice but remained miserable and suicidal for the next few years.

One day he sought solace in a welcoming church. While kneeling and sobbing in a pew, a priest approached him, and they spoke about his ordeal. The priest's best friend happened to be one of the best plastic surgeons in Australia, and he was impressed with the young man. The doctor performed free surgery on the disfigured man, and it was a miraculous success. Later in his life, the youth enjoyed tremendous success in show business, married and became a father. The story claims that the young man was Gibson and that this event was the inspiration for 1993's *The Man Without a Face*, which was obviously false, since the film is based on a 1972 novel.

In 1979 Gibson played the title character in Mad Max, *a film that takes place in the postapocalyptic future.*

ask you to believe a realistic relationship between a man and a woman one minute, and the next minute you're back in the comic strips. It mixed itself up a little, muddied its style, and nobody quite knew what to make of it."[26]

Other than most moviegoers, that is. *Mad Max* quickly became an international success, grossing $100 million worldwide, an astonishing amount at that time, and was even the most popular Australian film of 1979. For seven years afterward it stood as the biggest box-office draw of any Australian-made film (until 1986's *"Crocodile" Dundee* eclipsed it). In contrast, the film was an utter financial disaster in the United States. Adding insult to injury, American audiences didn't even hear Gibson's real voice. Mad Max's few lines were dubbed by another actor to avoid using Australian accents, which might be hard for Americans to follow.

Twenty-one years later Gibson would comment on *Mad Max*: "I was straight out of drama school. I didn't know what to think. I had virtually no experience with a real film. . . . *Mad Max* was made on a shoestring, but had the feel of an independent film you might see now."[27] Before the theatrical release of *Mad Max*, Gibson busied himself with his favorite kind of acting—theater. Joining the State Theatre Company of Australia, he was seen in small roles in everything from *Oedipus Rex* to Shakespeare's *Henry IV.*

As Gibson's career got off to a rollicking start, in Australia at least, his personal life was blooming as well. In 1978, while living in a boardinghouse in Adelaide, he met a pretty brunette nurse named Robyn Moore, who worked at the nearby Home for the Incurables. But there was an obstacle to the romantic potential: Robyn was dating someone. After a period of platonic friendship between Robyn and Mel, she and her boyfriend broke up. Soon after, Gibson and Moore began dating.

Love in the Air

In addition to Robyn and Mel's real life love match, his next role was that of the title character in the 1979 Australian film *Tim*. But as with *Summer City*, Gibson again fell into the role, when writer/director Michael Pate's son, Christopher, dropped out. Gibson did not disappoint Pate, who decided to take a chance on the still-unknown actor. In the drama Gibson portrays a mildly retarded handyman in love with an older woman (played by American actress Piper Laurie). Based on a novel by Colleen McCullough, the Australian-born author of *The Thorn Birds*, the film was released in the United States in 1981.

The role was an interesting departure in that Gibson would be playing more than just a fun-loving surfer dude or a leather-clad "cartoonish" desperado out for revenge. Tim Melville was more human, more real, and more dimensional, giving Gibson ample opportunity to display his dramatic range, unlike in *Summer City* and *Mad Max*. Much of the drama in the story has to do with the character of Mary (Laurie) falling in love with Tim and the events that take place in his family, including the death of his mother and his feelings of abandonment when his sister marries.

The actor has strong memories of his struggles with this early role, which was an important part of his career groundwork. "It was a challenging role," Gibson has said of Tim Melville. "But, early on I found a key into it: it wasn't so much playing someone retarded but rather stressing the innocence part of it—as if he were someone normal who had a link missing somewhere. I couldn't have played him drooling—it would've been a turn-off." His solution was to play Tim "like a puppy."[28]

From the beginning Gibson enjoyed a good reputation while working on *Tim* and exhibited a desire to learn and grow as an actor. "I can only tell you that every moment of the film working with Mel was a joy. I simply had to find a way to let Mel explore the possibilities of the part as I had written it," Pate later said in interviews.

Colleen McCullough wrote the novel Tim, *a story that was later adapted to a film starring Gibson.*

> He had told me in the first few days of filming that he had "never been directed" before, that all he could remember about *Mad Max*—true or false—was being told to stand here, look there, walk here. He really had very little film technique in those early days of *Tim*. But he took direction like a great big sponge; he learned very quickly and . . . very well. After all, the cast around him were all very experienced and competent film and TV performers.[29]

Piper Laurie revealed many years later that at the time she believed Gibson was indeed destined to be a star.

Although the film was successful, it was not a *Mad Max*–sized hit. Critics accused it of being "sappy." Still, *Tim* brought Gibson to the attention of the Australian Film Institute, which awarded him that year's Best Actor award. He was also recognized with a special honor called the Sammy Award for Best New Talent.

Just as Gibson began getting steady work and recognition, his relationship with Robyn Moore got serious. On June 7, 1980, they were married by the Reverend Clement Gailey in Forestville, New South Wales, where they exchanged simple gold wedding rings. The newlyweds could not afford a lavish honeymoon, so they stayed at a friend's home, just north of Sydney, instead. Within a few months, Robyn Gibson was expecting the couple's first child.

War Is Hell

With a new real-life role as a husband with a family to support, it was back to the boards of the stage for Mel Gibson. After taking on his true dramatic debut in *Tim*, a play called *No Names, No Pack Drill*, in which he played an American marine who goes AWOL, set the militaristic theme for his next two features as well.

First up was the World War II drama *Attack Force Z*, a movie Gibson would not speak of kindly in the years to follow, and that was on the few occasions he would discuss it at all.

> It was just a vulgar attempt at a war-action movie with Aussie WASPs shooting Chinese dressed up in Japanese uniforms. I don't like to talk about or even remember

that film. You do that kind of movie because you're starving to death. But there's something to be learned from doing almost anything. And the lesson I got from *Z-Men* [an alternate title used for the film] was never to do that again.[30]

Filmed in 1980, *Attack Force Z* would not be released for another two years in Australia, where it had a brief run in movie houses. Americans only encountered the film on cable or late-night TV, if at all.

Around 1977 Gibson had auditioned for a role in a movie called *The Last Wave*. The film was to be helmed by Peter Weir, a director who was carving out a place in Australian cinema for himself with the well-received films *The Cars That Ate Paris* (1974) and *Picnic at Hanging Rock* (1975). "I'm not going to cast you for this part," Weir told Gibson then. "You're not old enough. But thanks for coming in, I just wanted to meet you."[31] The starring role went to well-known film and TV actor Richard Chamberlain.

But in 1980 Weir had the right role for Gibson: that of soldier Frank Dunne in the battlefield drama *Gallipoli*, released the following year in the States. The film was set during the World War I battle at Gallipoli, near Istanbul. Australians—then British subjects—fought the Turks, who were German allies, with disastrous results: 26,000 Australians were wounded, and 7,594 were killed.

After seeing Gibson in *Mad Max*, director Weir knew the actor would make the perfect Frank, one of two professional runners who enlist in the military during the early part of World War I, albeit reluctantly on his character's part. "There are those guys who say 'I'm no coward; I'd go out and die for the country' and do. Frank didn't," Gibson told journalist Margaret Smith. "He had flashes of bravery, but only when there was no other choice."[32]

Weir was especially keen on Gibson for the part because he wanted him to represent the modern Australian as a survivor. Gibson, said Peter Weir, "*is* the new Australian."[33] The "new Australian" was not without his problems in the role of the runner Frank, though. For one thing, Gibson's smoking habit did

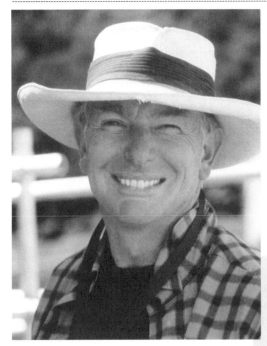

Director Peter Weir felt Gibson would be perfect for the role of Frank Dunne in the World War I battlefield drama Gallipoli.

not help when he was needed to run onscreen. For another, he weighed more than his costar, Mark Lee, which also slowed him down. But after undergoing a strict period of exercise, he was ready for the task.

And if *Gallipoli* was a test, Gibson passed it with flying colors. Critics loved the film, from *Film in Review*, to *Variety* and *Newsweek*, and they lavished praise on Gibson's solid performance as soldier Frank Dunne. *Gallipoli* was awarded nine Australian Film Institute Awards, including Best Picture, Best Director for Weir, and Best Actor for Gibson (his second such AFI award). The film was an unexpected hit with audiences too, especially in New York City, where a particular theater showed *Gallipoli* around the clock.

Significant developments occurred in Gibson's private life as well. While he listened by phone from the *Gallipoli* set in Egypt, Robyn Gibson gave birth to their first child, a daughter they named Hannah. The first-time father reacted with tears of joy. With his film credits growing, an ever-increasing paycheck, and an expanding family, it seemed that nothing could go wrong for Mel Gibson.

Chapter 3

Serious Actor, Serious Pressure

Aᴀғᴛᴇʀ ᴛʜᴇ ᴍᴏᴅᴇsᴛ successes of *Gallipoli* and *Tim*, Mel Gibson returned to his roots, specifically the character that had first brought him to the attention of Australian audiences. But this time it was different—this time American audiences would finally take notice as well. As a result of his growing celebrity, Gibson would discover, too, that fame sometimes comes with its downside, including time away from his expanding family, career disappointments, and an arrest on a drunk-driving charge.

The Road Stretches Forward

After appearing in a bit part in a little known flick called *Chain Reaction* with his friend Steve Bisley, Gibson returned to the future world of Mad Max Rockatansky in director George Miller's *Mad Max* sequel, *The Road Warrior* (1981).

Calling *The Road Warrior* "an act of atonement for *Mad Max*,"[34] Miller, who also cowrote the screenplay, set out to make a sequel that kept every bit that worked in the original film and make it that much better. The reception *The Road Warrior* received upon release seemed to affirm that he had accomplished just that. With an expanded budget of $4 million this time around, ten times more than *Mad Max*'s, Miller and producer Byron Kennedy could afford spectacular crash and chase scenes, which had become necessary sequences of any action movie at the time. The expanded budget of *The Road Warrior* was evidence of Gibson's growing fame in Australia and beyond and the continuing interest in the Max character.

The Road Warrior (some critics suggested that the title was changed from the one used Down Under—*Mad Max II*—to distance it from the original's box-office failure in America) follows the further adventures of Mad Max as he battles evil gang lords for what little gasoline is left on the war-ravaged earth. Coming upon a tiny refining community, he helps the inhabitants defend themselves against the feared Lord Humungus with the help of a child, known as Feral Kid, and a canine that Max simply calls "Dog."

Not much about the leather-clad vigilante Max had changed since the first film, but Gibson was enthusiastic about reprising the character from his first hit movie. "We approached him from the angle of the guy being like a closet human being," Gibson commented several years later. "He operates coldly because that's the only way to survive. It's down to basics. Eating dog food. Running for his life. You just live, you know. He doesn't even sneer. He's beyond that."[35] Some critics disagreed with Gibson's assessment, observing that he brought even more dimensions to his character the second time around.

The Road Warrior's Influence

In an interview with *Movieline* magazine in 2000, Gibson commented about *The Road Warrior:* "That one is really timeless. Very simple and powerful. All these ripoffs of it don't have the simplicity." When reminded by the interviewer that the film was still being liberally borrowed from, Gibson replied, "There was that one on the water [*Waterworld*]. *The Road Warrior*, though, was real simple and rough."

Countless critics have observed the influence of George Miller's 1981 classic film and its predecessor, *Mad Max. Waterworld* (1995), has not been the only film likened to it. Another Kevin Costner vehicle, *The Postman* (1997), also contains postapocalyptic elements reminiscent of *The Road Warrior*, as do the John Carpenter films *Escape from New York* (1981), and its sequel, *Escape from L.A.* (1996). Of the three *Mad Max* films, the first two—but especially *The Road Warrior*—have enjoyed the status of popular cult films over the years, meaning they have devoted fans who regard Max as the ultimate hero and *The Road Warrior* as the best movie of its genre. This popularity and fan devotion is one of the major reasons the *Max* films and the character have been such inspirations to other film makers.

The Road Warrior was a certified hit all over the world, including the United States, and Gibson's career continued at high pitch. Audiences and critics alike clamored for his next movie, and fan clubs devoted to the actor began to spring up all over the United States, Canada, and Australia. Yet twenty-seven-year-old Gibson, who was quickly becoming a well-known personality, was apprehensive about his newfound fame and fortune. By 1983, when his next movie was released, he commented in an interview, "Everything's been happening too fast. I've gotta put the brakes on here, or I'll smack into something."[36]

Living Dangerously

Gibson's concern with his burgeoning celebrity did not keep him from pursuing career opportunities that would fuel his fame. In 1982 he reteamed with *Gallipoli*'s director, Peter Weir, for another war drama, *The Year of Living Dangerously*. This film was the first to pair him with a hot Hollywood actress, in the person of *Alien* star Sigourney Weaver.

Set during the regime of the dictator Sukarno in Jakarta, Indonesia, in 1965, the film follows rookie Australian broadcaster Guy Hamilton, played by Gibson, on his first assignment as a radio journalist. Shortly after arriving in the politically restless country, Hamilton is befriended by Billy Kwan (played by actress Linda Hunt), a dwarf photographer. Hamilton is introduced to Weaver's Jill Bryant, a British friend of Kwan's, and she and Guy start a passionate relationship. Before long Guy is caught up in the very political tumult he is expected to merely observe for an Australian radio network.

Playing Guy Hamilton meant that Gibson, who had briefly wanted to be a journalist as a teenager, got to live like one for a while. To prepare for the part, Gibson spoke with several rough-and-tumble real-life journalists who had witnessed the fall of Sukarno firsthand. That didn't mean it was all play and no work getting into the passive character of Hamilton for Gibson, since the character only observes, and resists taking part in, most of the story developments. "It wasn't easy because he's not a character that initiates a lot. And you're on from the beginning to the end. . . . It's hard doing that puppet sort of part without being basically boring."[37]

In 1983, Sigourney Weaver starred with Gibson in The Year of Living Dangerously.

While filming in Manila in the Philippines, which stood in for Indonesia, the cast and crew truly were living on the edge of danger. Although everyone was assigned bodyguards, they were subject to repeated death threats from Muslim Philippine radicals, who thought the movie would insult their religion. Gibson later recalled this terrifying time:

> We were staying in this fabulous hotel. . . . And in the midst of all this civilized luxury we began getting death threats. The phone would ring and this bloke speaking in broken English would ask, "How brave are you, Mr. Gibson?" I'd say, "What do you want to know that for?" Then would come the threats—always something to do with bombs and death. The threats were real. They'd come in like clockwork and the phone would be

snatched off me by the bodyguard, who would start yab-
bering down the line in Tagalog, which is the native
tongue. Then he would slam down the phone and tell
me not to worry.

I worried. I wanted to leave right away, after the first
phone call. I've got a family, a real life, and this was only
a movie. I mean, there's nothing I won't do on screen to
put food on the table for my family. But when it comes
to my own life, I'm a pretty careful guy.[38]

After a five-week period of shooting in Manila, the production moved to Australia for the final week of filming. Gibson was
pleased with this development, since he and his wife welcomed
twin boys, Edward and Christian, on June 2, 1982, and he was
at the delivery in person this time. Just the same, he arrived on
the *Year* set on time the next morning.

*Linda Hunt won the
Oscar for Best Supporting
Actress for her portrayal of
a male photographer in*
The Year of Living
Dangerously.

Pairing Gibson with Weaver and supported by actress Linda Hunt, the 1983 Peter Weir film was lauded by critics upon release but failed to make a significant amount at the box office. Hunt, who with the director received the bulk of the accolades, was awarded a Best Supporting Actress Academy Award for her magnificent portrayal of a character of the opposite sex, Billy Kwan. Gibson's subtle performance did not go unnoticed, either. "Gibson, in his most demanding role to date, shows he's capable of achieving just about everything on screen," [39] declared one critic.

The Bounty

After *The Year of Living Dangerously*, Gibson was offered a part in the gangster film *Once Upon a Time in America*, which was to star Robert De Niro, but he turned down the role for the opportunity to perform as Biff Loman in an Australian stage production of *Death of a Salesman* in the fall of 1982. He was offered a role in 1983's *The Lords of Discipline*, too, but Gibson also declined that part because of his stage work and to try out for other pictures. During the same period, he auditioned for but did not win the role of composer Wolfgang Amadeus Mozart in *Amadeus*. The 1984 film later won Best Picture and seven other Oscars.

Although Gibson lost out on *Amadeus*, he remained busy, with three movies opening in 1984. And his sights were set on becoming a star in America, just as he was in his adopted homeland of Australia, since Hollywood offered a greater diversity of roles and more money. "After *The Road Warrior* my agent suggested I come over here and make films," Gibson told *Movieline* magazine in 2000. "I did and I worked in mediocre fare, films that had possibilities, but I just didn't have the maturity to help much. The people I was working with were all good and competent and I got to experiment, with minimal to moderate success." [40]

First up in '84 was *The Bounty*, an epic remake of *Mutiny on the Bounty* with Anthony Hopkins as Captain Bligh to Gibson's Fletcher Christian. The story of the revolt aboard the eighteenth-century British vessel *Bounty* had already been explored onscreen in 1935 and 1962, and Hollywood legends Clark Gable and Marlon Brando had previously played Christian. Comparisons were inevitable, but Gibson claimed he wasn't worried. "I didn't think much of the first effort. And Marlon Brando, who's he?" he joked to a journalist. But in all seriousness, Gibson said, "I'm confident. I have to be, or I could never have taken on the part."[41]

The Bounty's voyage to the big screen encountered problems from the start. First, the original director, David Lean, who had helmed such film masterpieces as *Lawrence of Arabia* and *The Bridge on the River Kwai*, dropped out of the production in its early stages. Then, although originally planned as a two-part series, the scripts were eventually condensed to make one feature. The film also differentiated itself from its earlier versions by portraying Captain Bligh as a sympathetic character for the first time. In this version Fletcher Christian, who led the tragic mutiny, was not the clear-cut hero of past versions. Gibson was attracted to the ambiguity and possibilities of Christian's character. "I even took some material on him to a London psychiatrist to find out just what sort of person he really was. He wasn't as lily-white as the public imagined him, nor was Bligh as bad."[42]

The Bounty, with its steamy scenes between Gibson and a topless island maiden, helped establish him as a true sex symbol in America. *People* magazine even named him its very first "Sexiest Man Alive." But Gibson was not totally comfortable with such labels. "It is because of the roles I've played. I don't mind it, in fact I find it rather flattering, but it's not really the way I want to be in real life."[43] Other times, Gibson complained about his and his family's loss of privacy while performing on the world stage, fearing that he was becoming "a target. . . . It's as if you have your pants down around your ankles and your hands tied behind your back. So here is a good opportunity for some parasite to come up from behind and throw some darts in your chest. Freedom of the press!"[44]

Coming to America

Clearly Gibson was having some conflicting issues with his growing celebrity, and the media's attention sometimes overwhelmed the actor. But that did not keep him from taking his first role in an American movie. In director Mark Rydell's *The River*, Gibson also played an American onscreen for the first time.

At first director Rydell was reluctant to hire Gibson to star as Tom Garvey, fearing his Australian accent would be obvious. But Gibson felt that he had to have the part, since farmer Tom Garvey, the quintessential American, could be his breakthrough with American audiences, critics, and Hollywood. Before leaving for England to film *The Bounty*, Gibson had asked Rydell not to cast *The River*'s male lead while Gibson studied with a vocal coach. When he returned months later, the director agreed to hire Gibson upon hearing his newly acquired southern twang. *The River* is the story of Tom and Mae Garvey, a family of farmers who fight against the odds to keep their land as a local river repeatedly threatens to destroy it. As if that did not pose enough of a struggle, a wealthy landowner wants the Garvey farm—and maybe Mae (Sissy Spacek), too.

Gibson was playing a family man on- and offscreen. Robyn Gibson and the children often accompanied the actor to the set in Holston Valley, Tennessee, and the entire family stayed in a spacious rented house in nearby Kingsport. This helped to anchor at least one aspect of Gibson's life—his personal life—

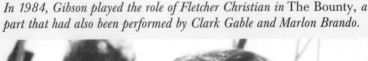

In 1984, Gibson played the role of Fletcher Christian in The Bounty, *a part that had also been performed by Clark Gable and Marlon Brando.*

In 1984, Gibson had an auto accident in Toronto (pictured) and was charged with impaired driving.

while his career underwent the major transition of moving into mainstream Hollywood features. And he was back on a farm for the first time since his family lived in Mount Vision, New York, in the '60s.

Gibson received high marks from Rydell, who called him "the star of the 1980s. I'm sure that he'll have more impact on the American film scene than anyone since James Dean or Marlon Brando. He has the roughness of a Steve McQueen or a Paul Newman and the sensitivity of a [Montgomery] Clift. He's an absolutely riveting performer. I don't think it's just physical beauty."[45]

Although critics, audiences, and the film industry were beginning to see that there surely was more to Gibson than his looks as he took on more dramatic roles, his next character shared that attribute and used it to his advantage. In 1984's *Mrs. Soffel*, Gibson was paired with another Academy Award–winning actress, Diane Keaton, in the true story of a romance between a convict and a prison warden's wife that led to a scandalous jailbreak in 1901 Pittsburgh.

Gibson once explained why he chose the project: As an actor with serious career goals, the challenge of "the bars" appealed to him. "It's a major dramatic device. You have a man and a woman and the way they relate, and you have an obstacle. The prison bars. It's interesting how they work to get around them, and eventually they lose the bars. There's always a good obstacle in a good love story."[46]

The entire Gibson family had arrived in Toronto, Canada, in January 1984 for the beginning of the film shoot, but many of Gibson's scenes were shot in other locations, outside the city. As a result, many times he would only see his wife and children on the weekends for the first two months. But by March, with filming dragging on and Robyn Gibson expecting the couple's fourth child, she and the children returned home, to Australia, where it was summer. The film began to run behind schedule, and by that time Gibson was only needed on the set about once a week. He increasingly grew bored and lonely, missing his family.

On April 25, 1984, his boredom caught up with him. Gibson was driving around Toronto in a rented car when he ran a red light and hit another vehicle. Although no one was hurt and the damage to the cars was minimal, the actor was given a Breathalyzer test, which showed that he was over the legal alcohol limit. He was arrested and charged with impaired driving. Calling home to report what happened, his wife demanded, "What the hell's the matter with you?"[47]

A week later, while his siblings celebrated his parents' fortieth wedding anniversary in Australia, Gibson appeared in a Toronto courtroom. Outside, throngs of female fans greeted the actor, who arrived forty-five minutes late for the scheduled hearing. One woman even tried to pass him her phone number. Gibson pleaded guilty to the charge of driving with over the legal eighty milligrams of alcohol in his bloodstream. His lawyer also told the court that Gibson, who had had no other trouble with the law, wanted to apologize to the court, the city, and the police officers who had handled his arrest. Gibson's sentence was then handed down: His Ontario driving privileges were suspended for a total of three months, and he was fined $300. The judge who imposed the sentence also seemed somewhat starstruck, as he wished Gibson an enjoyable stay in Canada.

Not long after, the cast and crew of *Mrs. Soffel* arrived in Pittsburgh, Pennsylvania, for some interior shots in the prison where the romance between Mrs. Soffel and the convict actually took place. After eight days in the city (instead of the scheduled five), filming was at long last completed, and the production left the city. An exhausted Gibson breathed a sigh of relief as the miserable shoot ended.

Although Gibson had made three dramatically respectable films, none were financially successful: *The River* and *The Bounty* both earned just over $8 million at theaters, with *Mrs. Soffel* making only about half that. Although he had received some praise for his roles, the films were box-office flops, and they often kept him from his wife and children. The growing pressures of stardom and a nonstop schedule had gotten to Gibson, and he aimed to remedy the situation. His plans for the rest of 1984 were to return home to Australia and take a break.

Chapter 4

Blockbuster!

Struggling to put the disappointments and harried work schedule of 1984 behind him, Gibson entered a stabilizing period in his life. Maturing as an actor, a husband, and a father, and sobering up—at least temporarily—Gibson enjoyed a winning streak as he established himself as one of the most sought-after actors in movies. While 1984 had been a year of failures and life lessons, the next few years offered the chance to redeem himself—to his family, his fans, and himself.

There's No Place Like Home

After shooting on *Mrs. Soffel* had ended, Gibson returned to the family home in Coogie Beach, Australia, just before Robyn Gibson gave birth to their fourth child, William, in June 1984. For the next three months, Gibson enjoyed the comforts of home away from the pressures of moviemaking, spending quality time with his wife and children and performing the normal activities of a husband and father. He also reconnected with his father, Hutt Gibson, with whom he tore down and rebuilt a cottage on his property. This was important, since his drunk-driving arrest had disappointed not just his wife but also his parents, who always strove to keep their children on the right paths in life. The incident "really woke Mel up," Anna Gibson later said. "He realized he'd let the beer take hold. The boy changed after that. I was particularly happy no one got hurt in the transition. It could have been tragic."[48]

Before long, though, he would be back at work, this time on the third installment of the *Mad Max* series. With the success of *The Road Warrior* fresh in their minds and the leading

Gibson teamed up with music legend Tina Turner in Mad Max Beyond Thunderdome, *the third installment in the Mad Max series.*

man receiving plenty of attention—most of it good—Hollywood producers came calling for the film that would make George Miller's Max trilogy complete, *Mad Max Beyond Thunderdome.* Along with Gibson's star power, though, there would be the addition of music legend Tina Turner, who was enjoying a major career comeback with the album *Private Dancer* and its hit singles after almost a decade out of the public eye. She had been signed to fill the role of the film's villainess, Aunty Entity.

Gibson was initially reluctant to make the 1985 release after the pressure of making three films back-to-back and only a short time off. The previous year he had worked "too much—I pigged out: three movies," he told a journalist. "I guess I was hungry to work. But I'm becoming very satisfied, to the point of being bloated."[49] Still, he looked forward to visiting Mad Max Rockatansky again, and he was paid $1 million for the role. "We're working in a new area with this one," he said at the time. "Had this been just a remake of *Road Warrior*, I wouldn't have done it. What would be the point? But this is a much more human story, even though it has that same kinetic energy. . . . In this one, [Max's] protective layers are peeled away. There's a lot more depth, variety, and humanity to the man."[50]

Gibson's drinking continued during the shooting of *Thunderdome*. What's more, the production began under a stifling sun in the Australian opal-mining city of Coober Pedy—temperatures sometimes reached as high as 104 degrees—in September 1984. Even a reporter from *People* magazine noticed the sometimes tense on-set climate created by Gibson's drinking, mixed with the oppressive heat and his initial hesitation to make the film.

Gibson later admitted that

> sometimes I fought so hard and drank so much that I surprised even myself. But there were so many people hanging around me, assuring me I could do anything I wanted, that I believed them. I'd wake up in the morning with no idea where the hell I'd been the night before. And then I'd get dressed, stagger out and not know where the hell I was gonna finish up.[51]

He blamed his alcoholic binges on his history of drinking when he was teenager, which first resurfaced during the filming of *The Bounty*, and on missing his wife and children. The production even employed a driver and a "baby-sitter" to keep an eye on the star, just so they could avoid another incident like the one in Toronto only a few months earlier. Surprisingly, while Gibson's drinking continued, he was a professional in every other sense, including arriving on the set on time, memorizing his lines, and giving a solid performance.

During this time Turner challenged Gibson about his problem. His *Thunderdome* costar sent him a glossy photograph of himself with the words "Don't screw this up" written over his face, prompting him to seriously think about quitting drinking, which he did—for a while. "It was quite a loving gesture," he later told *Ladies' Home Journal* about what his costar had done. "She was a woman of far greater experience than myself, and it really made me stop and think."[52]

When the four-month shoot ended, Gibson headed back home for more badly needed rest and time with the family. When *Mad Max Beyond Thunderdome* opened in the summer of 1985, Gibson was treated to his first hit movie in three years— since the last *Mad Max* film, *The Road Warrior. Thunderdome* earned $36 million—a solid take and the most any of his movies had made so far.

Lethal Box-Office Weapon

After the completion of *Thunderdome,* Gibson again retreated to his newly acquired farm in Kiewa Valley, Australia, where he enjoyed leisure time with his family and attempted to live the life of a farmer, even going so far as to neuter the ranch's bulls himself. After more than a year off, he received the script for *Lethal Weapon,* and he was immediately interested in playing the role of suicidal, loose-cannon cop Martin Riggs.

The part of Riggs was different from most of those he had been offered around that time, he said in a later interview.

> At that time, there was this plethora of films about muscle-bound dudes who were two-dimensional. They saved the world, but they weren't real at all. *Lethal Weapon* is about a person who's been through war, who assassinates people for a living and is on a police force. What does all that do to him? The guy's suicidal. I hadn't seen that [before].[53]

Gibson had even turned down a role similar to the ones he spoke of, the title character in *The Running Man,* which eventually went to Arnold Schwarzenegger.

A meeting was set up between Danny Glover, who was being considered for the costarring role of the stable, family man and homicide detective Roger Murtaugh, director Richard Donner, and Gibson in Los Angeles in 1986. Donner was impressed with the interaction between the two actors, and a deal was made. Later that year, family in tow, Gibson temporarily moved to Los Angeles for production of *Lethal Weapon.* He was previously quoted as saying that he would never live in Los Angeles, but as Gibson's star began to rise, the likelihood of commuting from Australia seemed less and less feasible.

Glover and Gibson, who had first met several months earlier at an airport in Venice, Italy, did not immediately bond. The reason for this was their different approaches to acting. Gibson, always a staunch anti-Method actor, was paired with a disciple of the style in his costar. Eventually, though, the two actors forged a partnership that mirrored itself onscreen, as cops Murtaugh and Riggs, partners unified by their past as Vietnam War vets, become allies during the course of the film.

Before meeting Gibson, director Donner had harbored the fear that Gibson might be just the opposite kind of performer

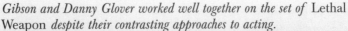
Gibson and Danny Glover worked well together on the set of Lethal Weapon *despite their contrasting approaches to acting.*

than what he is. "I was expecting to have problems with him," he has said. "I thought he was going to be a Method actor, somebody who wanted to know where everything came from and why. But give him one word and he runs with it. Half the time he doesn't even need that."[54] As a result, things ran smoothly on the *Lethal Weapon* shoot.

By all accounts, *Lethal Weapon*'s was a pleasant set, though it did get a bit tense when Riggs attempts suicide. In one take Gibson clinched the scene and relayed his character's desperation so well that cast and crew members were getting choked up watching the camera monitors. Even the star himself actually cried while shooting that wrenching moment. The film was demanding in a physical sense too, since it climaxed with Gibson's character in a violent martial arts match with the villain Mr. Joshua, played by veteran actor Gary Busey. The sequence took four full nights to film in drenching rain. Earlier, in preparation for their roles, Gibson and Glover had observed some real-life Los Angeles detectives, but Gibson was hesitant to get involved in any actual police situations, since the star, husband, and father

The atmosphere on the set of Lethal Weapon *was tense at times.*

of four had recently turned thirty years old. "I noticed that things aren't what they used to be; after that third decade you've got to be careful,"[55] he was quoted as saying on the set.

Although reviews were generally mixed, the movie earned its share of praise. Critic Jeffrey Lyons compared *Lethal Weapon* to the well-regarded 1971 action thriller *The French Connection.* Audiences let it be known that they loved the film, as ticket sales rang up more than $65 million in the United States and almost double that figure worldwide. Even before production was completed on *Lethal Weapon,* a sequel was being planned by its studio, Warner Bros., and director Richard Donner. But before that, Gibson would become a father for the fifth time, with the birth of son Louis, and he would make another Hollywood production with very famous costars.

Tequila Sunrise

After the hit *Lethal Weapon* was released, Mel Gibson was the name on the lips of most casting agents and directors in Hollywood, and the now high-profile star was flooded with scripts. The problem was that most were knockoffs of *Weapon,* and Gibson wanted to avoid typecasting. He also aimed to go beyond the "Sexiest Man Alive" designation that he'd been carrying for several years. In essence, he wanted to go beyond the Martin Riggs and Mad Max characters and play a real character with real emotions and flaws.

In 1988, *Tequila Sunrise* was written by *Chinatown* scribe Robert Towne, who also directed, and the project interested Gibson from the first time he read the script. He would be costarring with two of Hollywood's hottest actors at the time, Michelle Pfeiffer and Kurt Russell. But one thing about the role of Dale McKussic bothered Gibson: He was a former drug dealer. Gibson, even though he still fought his alcoholic demons and his on-again, off-again cigarette habit, was not sure he should accept the part, since he found the character's business morally objectionable. To get into his character's mind-set (as he had done with the Martin Riggs character in *Lethal Weapon*), Gibson spent time talking with a former drug dealer and came away with the feeling that *Tequila Sunrise* depicted good and evil on a realistic spectrum, rather than in a simplified,

Legendary Prankster

Since at least *Lethal Weapon*, Gibson has been known as a notorious on-set joker. After filming his character's near-suicide scene in that film, Gibson attached a red clown nose to his face to break the tension. Other times he has been prone to belch out loud for the same purpose.

While costarring with Julia Roberts in 1997's *Conspiracy Theory*, Gibson sent the beautiful actress a gift-wrapped freeze-dried rat as a present, which brought horrific shrieks from Roberts's trailer. (Roberts later retaliated by carefully wrapping his toilet seat in Saran Wrap.) Another time he showed up at *Forever Young* costar Jamie Lee Curtis's door wearing a hockey mask and wielding a knife, bringing back her memories of being an '80s horror queen from her stint in the *Halloween* movies. And during the production of 2000's *The Patriot*, he continued his comic antics. When director Roland Emmerich celebrated a birthday, Gibson hired the Carolina Panthers cheerleaders to sing him "Happy Birthday," which was followed by the film's extras giving a salute of their own: They mooned Emmerich, just as William Wallace's troops did to the British in a famous *Braveheart* scene.

In a 2000 interview, Michael Fleming of *Movieline* magazine asked if Gibson had decided to mature. "I think so," Gibson answered. "Or I'm just getting slower."

clear-cut fashion. He accepted the McKussic role, feeling that it would be an interesting test of his acting skills and a departure from his role as "hero."

Revolving around the complicated relationship between McKussic, his friend, who is a Los Angeles cop (played by Russell), and the woman (Pfeiffer) who comes between them, the flick further cemented Gibson's sex-symbol status and made him a magazine-cover fixture. In the end *Tequila Sunrise* ended up with a box-office take of $41 million, making it a relative dud, but it did nothing to dampen the public's appetite for more Gibson movies, including the sequel to 1987's *Lethal Weapon*.

More Lethal than Ever

Less than two years after the original film premiered, the cast and crew found themselves back in Los Angeles filming *Lethal Weapon 2*, which still holds the record as the most successful en-

Joe Pesci helped bring a humorous tone to the production of Lethal Weapon 2.

try in the series, making an astonishing $147 million at the U.S. box office alone. In his *Movie & Video Guide*, noted film critic Leonard Maltin calls *Lethal Weapon 2* "a must for action fans."[56]

The 1989 flick finds Riggs and Murtaugh, still partners, on the trail of a South African drug lord protected by his diplomatic credentials. It also features the addition of a comedic Joe Pesci to the cast, and the tone was definitely becoming more humorous and less tense than its predecessor. The lighter mood includes a less-brooding Riggs and hilarious mayhem, like the scene involving Murtaugh's toilet, which has been rigged to explode—a plot development credited to Gibson and his desire to bring more fun to his character and to the film series. Another aspect included in this *Weapon* and missing from the first: a love interest for Riggs, in the person of British actress Patsy Kensit as the diplomat's assistant.

Critics, notoriously dismissive of most action-adventure films, were no different this time, with the exception of the highly regarded *New York Times*. Its critic lauded the film, commenting that "Gibson, Donner and Glover have concocted the best action-buddy-comedy formula since *Butch Cassidy and the Sundance Kid*"[57]—high praise indeed.

After beginning the 1980s as the popular leather-clad hero of *The Road Warrior* and trying his hand at American films, although unsuccessfully at first, Gibson now enjoyed superstar status in the United States and around the world. He could do anything he wanted to in the movie business. Within a year that would include taking the riskiest role of his career.

Chapter 5

Power Player

AFTER MULTIPLE HIT movies, by the end of the '80s Gibson was able to pick and choose projects as he pleased. By 1990 the now marketable and powerful star—whose name above the title of a movie guaranteed it plenty of attention and, most of the time, lots of money—shocked the entertainment industry and earned its respect when he decided to break out of the action-star mold and tackle one of the great works of dramatic theater.

Capers and High Jinks

After taking on Martin Riggs's sometimes-unbalanced personality for a second time, Gibson signed up for a movie that was a complete genre change from his last few films and a departure from his previous résumé in general. His first comedy, 1990's *Bird on a Wire*, costarred Goldie Hawn, longtime girlfriend of Gibson's *Tequila Sunrise* pal Kurt Russell. During the filming of *Sunrise*, the Gibsons and Russell and Hawn had become quite friendly, and when the *Bird* script surfaced, Gibson and Hawn decided the project was the right one to match them up as a team. The *Bird on a Wire* set was extremely family friendly, with the Gibson children frequently found in close proximity with Hawn's. Robyn Gibson even announced her sixth pregnancy on the set of the film, which was celebrated with a champagne toast.

Gibson had been looking for a comedy role for some time, and with the addition of veteran funny woman Hawn, he felt the time and the project were right. Gibson reflected on his desire to act in different genres in a 2000 interview with *Venice* magazine: "I think variety is the spice of life and I like to hop around and do different things. There's a smorgasbord out there to be had if you can take advantage of it."[58]

Gibson starred with Kurt Russell (right) in 1988's Tequila Sunrise *and with Goldie Hawn (left) in 1990's* Bird on a Wire.

The star maintains a sense of humor about his first comedy. Today Gibson jokes that *"Bird on a Wire* was one of my finest works. Oscar caliber."[59] Few would agree with that assessment, but few would also deny that the caper film was a relatively harmless chase flick centering around Gibson's character, an FBI-protected witness being hunted by killer drug runners. Complicating matters and providing much of the comedy is the reappearance of his former lover, played by Hawn.

Bird on a Wire did well at the box office, making about $5 million more than the first *Lethal Weapon*, demonstrating Gibson's growing appeal with audiences. The picture also marked the first time that Gibson had set foot in Canada, where *Bird* was filmed, since his 1984 drunk-driving arrest. Although critics were generally negative, one did single out Gibson's witty performance, saying, "It was an indescribably bad film, but Mel came out of it okay."[60] Gibson's follow-up to *Bird on a Wire* would be a different story.

A Rare Flop

Although Gibson's career was riding high in the several years after *Lethal Weapon*, he encountered his share of professional disappointments. In later years Gibson would say of his next film,
"It was a good script, and it didn't translate on-screen at all. I
don't really know why. I have my theories, but I don't want to
besmirch anybody. I remember watching it and thinking,
'Whoa, that wasn't too good.'"[61] Audiences and critics seemed to
agree with the star regarding his second 1990 film, *Air America*,
for which he reportedly received a salary of $4.2 million. Based
on the true story of a covert airline that operated out of the na-
tion of Laos during the Vietnam War, the film was a hot property in its early development stages, which attracted Gibson in
the first place.

There were plenty of challenges to making *Air America*. First
was Gibson's dislike of flying, which he controlled through flying lessons before the start of production. Second, the Gibsons
were expecting again, and he was not sure he would make it
home for the birth, since filming would take place in the remote
jungles of Thailand for four months. Third, though perhaps
most important, danger lurked close to the set, since the area

Reluctant Superstar

Although Gibson is the highest-paid actor in movie history, enjoys im-
measurable fame and wealth, and is admired by millions of fans around
the world, he has sometimes confessed to being uncomfortable with
his celebrity—and what comes with it, including unwanted attention
to his personal life and an occasional lack of privacy for him and his
family. He once confessed about interviews, "I've never gotten used to
this part of the process. It's unnatural. I'm never comfortable."

On another occasion he defended himself when he felt that he was
portrayed by the press and liberal groups as something he feels he is
not. "It's baffling that people define me as a right-wing misogynist. I
haven't been married for 20 years by being a caveman," he remarked.

All in all, Gibson is philosophical about and grateful for the life he
leads, but when *Entertainment Weekly* once asked him what he would
do if he were the most powerful person in entertainment, he answered, "I'd move out of Hollywood and begin a new life."

was under the control of a big-time drug dealer. (According to one account, the filmmakers and the drug dealer were able to keep the peace after Gibson autographed some memorabilia, which then was given to the enthusiastic *Mad Max* fan.)

Though Sean Connery and Kevin Costner were first mentioned for the roles of a veteran pilot and his younger counterpart, they were apparently out of the filmmakers' budget. Gibson was subsequently cast as the younger of the two pilots, but he ultimately felt he was too old for the part, which then went to Robert Downey Jr. Instead, Gibson became the older pilot.

Watching rushes, the film from each day's shooting, with the director, Robert Spottiswoode, Gibson could see that *Air America* might not live up to his expectations and others'. Increasing his stress level, he was trying to kick his cigarette habit. But he still drank, after several failed attempts at quitting. He was homesick for his wife and children and concerned about the sixth child on the way.

Toward the end of the making of the movie in Asia, Robyn Gibson went into labor, but her husband could not be there. This reportedly upset Gibson so much that he boycotted the taking of the cast-and-crew picture at the end of the *Air America* shoot, despite his friendly relationships with many of his colleagues on the film. Gibson had to settle for his oldest child, Hannah, describing the birth of her brother Milo over the phone. The *Air America* shoot had been a challenge, but Gibson was in for an even greater test—the one his whole career could be riding on.

To Be or Not to Be

While watching Gibson's acting during the suicide attempt scene from 1987's *Lethal Weapon*, prominent Italian stage and film director Franco Zeffirelli was impressed. He knew he had found the actor who could play Hamlet in his long-planned film of the revered Shakespearean play. But first he had to convince Gibson to take the risk of playing one of the most challenging roles ever written.

At first Gibson was hesitant. If *Hamlet* failed onscreen, he could be a laughingstock of the movie business. Barring all un-

Gibson's agent Ed Limato, shown here with Diana Ross, dissaproved of Gibson's desire to play the role of Hamlet.

certainties, he was intrigued, especially since he felt the need to expand his range as a performer and take on something more varied than the action-adventure heroes he had been playing for much of the last few years. In a later interview with *Biography Magazine*, he discussed why he thought he needed to play the melancholy prince of Denmark: "I think people had preconceptions. . . . I'm more suited to certain types of archetypal characters—the hero/leader-guy—and therefore I was typecast into that role. And that's okay. But it's good to depart from it, for your own sanity. Otherwise it's like being on a merry-go-round: You keep going in circles, never getting anywhere."[62]

When Gibson and Zeffirelli announced their plans to make the 1990 film, they found others had their doubts about the future film's success. Warner Bros., the company that wanted to tie Gibson into a long-term contract, was nervous, and so was the actor's agent, Ed Limato, who expressed his disapproval. Eventually, Warner Bros., the studio behind the *Lethal Weapon* franchise, helped finance the film with the support of the star's new production company, Icon Productions, which was founded around this time. (This was Gibson's second company set up to generate film vehicles for himself and other actors. The first, Lovell-Gibson, folded in 1989 before getting any projects off the ground.) Gibson also agreed to take a pay cut for *Hamlet*, reportedly earning less than $1 million for the role.

The people who were most pessimistic about the challenge that lay ahead of Gibson did not realize that before becoming one of the top box-office draws in the world, he had done more than his share of Shakespeare. His Romeo to Judy Davis's Juliet while at NIDA had been one of his standout performances at the school, and he had also acted in a production of *Henry IV*. Gibson's diverse choice of roles over the years also proved that he was hungry to go beyond people's perceptions of him. Gibson admitted his concerns about the role during this time. "There are moments playing Hamlet that make you want to rip your hair out because he is the most confounding character ever written. The only consistent thing about Hamlet is his inconsistency, and you're chasing your tail. You feel like you're going mad—and you do, a little bit."[63]

Besides the enormity of taking on perhaps Shakespeare's most exalted work, Gibson would also be walking in the footsteps of some renowned actors, including Laurence Olivier and Derek Jacobi, a situation he had first encountered while playing Fletcher Christian in *The Bounty*. Unfortunately, he made an unsuccessful attempt to give up smoking again to help with his breathing while reciting the play's monologues, all the while endeavoring to learn how to skillfully sword fight and ride a horse. Beyond mastering the physical activities of *Hamlet*, Gibson further proved his dedication to the project by growing a beard and dyeing his hair blond for the first time since *Summer City*. At first the studio was adverse to the idea of having *Hamlet*'s star change his immediately recognizable look, but it eventually backed down.

Easing the frustration a bit was the stellar cast with which Zeffirelli surrounded the star, including Glenn Close as Hamlet's mother, Gertrude, along with Helena Bonham Carter, Alan Bates, and Ian Holm. Keeping his wife, Robyn, and their children close by also helped; even Hutt and Anna Gibson flew into England for part of the shooting to be near their son as he took this important step in his career.

Support also came by way of Gibson's costars. "Mel Gibson is brilliant. He is going to surprise a lot of people," said Alan Bates, the film's Claudius, Hamlet's murderous uncle and stepfather. "It's a hell of a thing for a mega-star of his magnitude to put himself on the line playing Hamlet with a lot of Brits," Ian Holm declared. "He does just fine."[64] The supportive words of his fellow thespians almost certainly buoyed Gibson's spirits and quieted any dismissal of his acting skills.

While *Hamlet* was under way, developments occurred with Gibson's other two 1990 pictures. Journalists had to be flown onto the *Hamlet* set to interview Gibson about *Bird on a Wire*, which had just opened, costing the studio thousands of dollars. Then, reshoots were ordered for *Air America*. The movie had not gone over well with test audiences, and it was decided that a different ending would improve it. The producers of that film had to wait until the *Hamlet* production was over, since Gibson had undergone such a physical transformation to play the Dane, so they could film a new scene featuring Gibson and costar Robert Downey Jr.

Earning Respect

As for *Hamlet*, the gamble seemed to pay off for Gibson. While the film did not make much money, it did show audiences, the film industry, and critics that Gibson was able to stretch as a thespian. "Gibson has never been more impressive," one film reviewer wrote. "His performance is intelligent, superbly physical and totally free of poetic posturing."[65] The *New York Post* chimed in: "Mel Gibson makes a very good Hamlet. It's a doubly pleasant surprise since we've had to judge him by the likes of *Mad Max* and *Lethal Weapon*."[66] It had been a successful start for Icon Productions and Gibson's first foray into producing, too.

One sad footnote to *Hamlet* has to do with Gibson's mother. Just as the picture was set to premiere in the United States in

December 1990, Anna Gibson, who had been plagued with several serious ailments, died of a heart attack. Missing the premiere and a scheduled live appearance on Phil Donahue's talk show, Gibson rushed home to Australia to join the rest of his siblings in offering the final farewell to their patient, good-natured mother. Gibson was said to be especially devastated, since his mother would never get to see his impressive *Hamlet* performance onscreen. Ever dedicated to his work, Gibson returned to Los Angeles only a few days later to continue promoting the Zeffirelli film.

After *Hamlet*'s debut, Gibson returned to Australia and his alma mater, NIDA, to promote a technical/creative scholarship that bears his name and to encourage the students at his former school. Australian critics were equally impressed with his acting in *Hamlet*; indeed, British critics seemed the only ones to find much fault with the film. Regardless, Gibson was honored in 1991 by Washington, D.C.'s Shakespeare Theatre, which awarded him its annual William Shakespeare Award for Classical Theatre (commonly called the Will Award) for his performance in *Hamlet*.

Lethal Weapon 3

After 1989's *Lethal Weapon 2*, Gibson claimed that he would never make another *Lethal Weapon*. Coming off his successful interpretation of *Hamlet*, he was getting tired of being typecast as an action star. Hollywood producer Joel Silver called Gibson at his farm Down Under and convinced him to reprise the Riggs character for the 1992 film. Gibson liked the fun script—and the reported $10 million fee—and signed on.

The third installment, which the star later admitted had some plot holes, finds Danny Glover's character, Roger Murtaugh, on the eve of his retirement from the police force, when he and Riggs are caught up in a plot involving a cop-turned–illegal firearms dealer. Gibson's real-life pal Joe Pesci was back as shifty Leo Getz, and Riggs also entered a love-hate relationship with an internal affairs officer, played by Rene Russo.

As usual, critics were unimpressed, but Gibson and the film-makers had the last laugh when *Lethal Weapon 3* made a very healthy $300 million around the world. Although *Lethal Weapon 3* didn't earn many critical raves, it kept Gibson's star high in the horizon and kept his fans satisfied until his next movie.

Forever Young

In 1991, while taking some time off to be with his loved ones, Gibson made an important choice in his life. At the urging of both his wife, Robyn, and manager, Ed Limato, he reportedly joined Alcoholics Anonymous, finally giving up alcohol for good. A decade later he discussed his reasons for getting sober once and for all: "You have to think about what's right and what the priorities are, and you have to take better care of yourself so you're around when [your family] need[s] you. It's not just all about you anymore—there are people who depend on you. So

Rene Russo played the role of an internal affairs officer who has a love-hate relationship with Gibson's character in Lethal Weapon 3.

it was a wake-up call of sorts."[67] Gibson rededicated himself to playing the family man and slowed the pace of his career after the busy last few years.

Refreshed after a year-long hiatus and ready to work again, Gibson chose a project that Icon Productions and Warner Bros. had acquired for him. Eager to make another romantic—rather than excessively violent—picture, the screenplay, first titled *The Rest of Daniel*, seemed to be just what Gibson was searching for at the time. Eventually the 1992 movie's title was changed to *Forever Young,* and Jamie Lee Curtis and Elijah Wood were brought on board to costar.

Forever Young is the whimsical, slightly far-fetched tale of a heartbroken pilot (Gibson) who volunteers to undergo cryogenic freezing when his fiancée, injured in an accident, falls into a coma. More than fifty years later, he is accidentally reawakened by a couple of mischievous young boys. Soon, he finds out that his fiancée is still alive, and he sets out to find her.

Elijah Wood and Gibson starred in Forever Young, *a film about a pilot who sets out to find his fiancée after having been cryogenically frozen for years.*

Although the film was lambasted by most critics, some praised the winning cast, and *Forever Young* made a fair amount at the box office—$55 million in the United States and $100 million worldwide. On the strength of his performances in *Hamlet* and *Forever Young*, Warner Bros., eager to keep Mel, signed the actor to a lucrative long-term contract. All told, the deal was rumored to be worth $100 million to Gibson, whose Icon Productions would produce several of the features.

In just a few short years, Gibson had gone from bankable star to guaranteed draw, and he had become one of the highest-paid actors in Hollywood, earning approximately $12 million per motion picture. With the title of producer also on his résumé, the next step in his career seemed logical for the ambitious Gibson: He hoped to direct his first film.

Chapter 6

A New Role

AFTER CONQUERING THE challenge of *Hamlet* onscreen as both actor and producer, only a strong directing debut by Gibson could further impress the film industry—an achievement he would garner three years later. But it was to be his second feature as director, *Braveheart*, that proved his first success was no fluke and brought him some of the film industry's highest honors. On a less positive note, this film would also bring him some negative press, as Gibson became embroiled in a very public war of words with the gay community, which had been displeased with some of his comments and actions since the early '90s.

The Man Without a Face

Since around 1990 Gibson's interest had been piqued by the idea of directing a motion picture, and the staff at Icon Productions had been searching for just such a project. At first producers offered him 1992's *Forever Young* as his directorial debut, but Gibson decided against it. He wanted to make the leap to the director's chair with something a bit more intimate in scope and with a smaller budget. In that way, the focus would then be on the film itself and his work as a director—not just the picture's success or failure at the box office.

Along came an adaptation of a 1972 novel, *The Man Without a Face*. Gibson considered it the perfect directorial debut since it fit his requirements, but he decided against performing double duty by starring in the picture as well as directing. The problem was that no one else wanted the role. "I was my fourth choice for the role,"[68] he has said. So he eventually took the part of former teacher Justin McLeod, a recluse horribly disfigured in an accident, who develops a special bond with a fatherless boy (Nick Stahl), to the suspicion of the boy's family and the townspeople, who think the man's motives may be less than fatherly. (The movie differed from the novel, in which the teacher and the young man, Chuck Norstadt, become lovers.)

Initially studio executives were hesitant to let Gibson star with half of his instantly recognizable face under mounds of disfiguring makeup (just as they had been with the blond hair and beard he had adopted for *Hamlet*), but they relented. "I guess I was naive because I didn't think it would be a problem, which it was. If [the film] had cost a lot of money, they would have said no,"[69] Gibson admitted in an interview seven years later.

While Gibson was excited by the idea of helming his first movie, he was also terrified at the prospect. He sought the advice of actor/director Clint Eastwood, who advised Gibson not

In 1993 Gibson made his directorial debut with The Man Without a Face.

to minimize the importance of what he had subconsciously learned on film sets over the years. When he confided to *Gallipoli* and *The Year of Living Dangerously* director Peter Weir that he was "really scared," Weir responded, "You'd *better* be scared!"[70] The first-time director later explained to interviewers that he had been inspired to direct through watching the techniques of Weir and George Miller, especially.

The actor sees directing like "flying blind. You kind of know where you want it to go but you're not sure the direction to take that will get you there. But if you work with enough great directors, guys like [the *Lethal Weapons'*] Dick Donner, you learn from them. I'm like Mr. Sponge Boy—I absorb everything."[71] As an actor who was directing, Gibson was also extra attentive to his cast members and open to their suggestions, since he had first-hand appreciation of the work ahead of them.

The Man Without a Face was filmed with an approximate budget of $12 million in the towns of Camden and Bayside, Maine, which provided the picturesque seaside scenery in the film. Reports indicated a happy set, and members of the cast had plenty of compliments for their director. Unfortunately, directing and acting in the movie sometimes became too much to bear, and Gibson was rumored to occasionally fall asleep in midsentence during shooting, despite his habit of downing coffee drinks—instead of alcohol—at the local café.

After production completed in Maine, Gibson and his family traveled to the South of France, where he edited the film away from the pressures of the industry. When *The Man Without a Face* opened in August 1993, most critics were impressed. *Entertainment Weekly* gave the film a grade of B-, while the *Los Angeles Times* called *The Man Without a Face* "a quality, intelligent production—a moving and substantial achievement."[72] Leonard Maltin, too, was positive about Gibson's presentations both behind and in front of the camera. "Despite several dramatic lapses, Gibson's directorial debut is more than respectable; he and Stahl offer excellent performances,"[73] the critic wrote in his respected *Movie & Video Guide*.

Daunting as the task was, Gibson was pleased with his first effort as director. He was also appreciative of the piece's mes-

Gibson's double duty for Braveheart *included directing the film and performing the lead role of William Wallace.*

sage, which hit close to home. "In my business, we're judged on appearances first," he said at the time. "My movie is about looking past appearances to test the real worth of people."[74] And with *The Man Without a Face*, Mel Gibson had proven that acting was not his only talent.

Braveheart

Just before the release of 1994's Western adventure *Maverick*, Gibson again turned his attention to feature-film directing. After the success of his directorial debut, he was eager to helm another motion picture. In the spring of 1994, the six-month-long *Braveheart* production began in Scotland.

As with *The Man Without a Face*, Gibson had initially declined to take the lead role, only to end up playing the character.

He believed he was too old to play the Scottish revolutionary William Wallace, known to his people as "Braveheart" for his resistance to English rule. The film's producers disagreed, and Gibson performed double duty on the epic motion picture, something he never planned to attempt again after his 1993 movie and something he vows he will never do in the future. To this day Gibson refuses to divulge the name of the actor that he wanted to play Wallace. All he would say in a 2000 interview was that "the person I wanted wasn't big enough at that time, and the studio wouldn't accept him."[75]

The epic's war sequences were a major concern to the second-time director, who worked with a budget estimated between $40 and $70 million. Before shooting began, Gibson asked his assistant to compile battle scenes from vintage Hollywood films for him to study. "I said, 'Okay, we've got to go beyond all this stuff,'" he later told a journalist.

> I think the nearest I saw to what I wanted was in Orson Welles' *Chimes at Midnight* (1966). It was black and white and there were some neat aspects to the battle scenes that he really made work, even though he had a very low budget. . . . So I went from everything I saw and then tried to make it my own way. I looked at these illustrations that depicted these massive confrontations of the period, and it was just claustrophobic and in your face, horses falling over on people, just a mess.[76]

The production later moved to Ireland, where scores of army reservists served as extras, to film several battle scenes.

Braveheart's onscreen battles were not the only challenge to making the epic. One crew member told a journalist that the movie was "organized chaos from start to finish. The weather was appalling, the accommodation was pretty awful but throughout the shoot cast and crew worked together, ate together and [socialized] together, which is very unusual on a big Hollywood movie."[77] Much of the camaraderie on the set was credited to director Gibson, who throughout his career has always positively interacted with cast and crew at all levels. Gibson was able to draw capable performances from the international cast, which also included Sophie Marceau, Patrick McGoohan, and Catherine McCormack, and the nearly three-hour film was released in May 1995. The film's slow start at the box office began to build, fueled by word of mouth and critical acclaim from the *New York Times*, *Los Angeles Magazine*, and other influential publications.

The following winter *Braveheart* was nominated for several Golden Globe Awards, and Gibson collected a statuette as Best Director. But many in the film industry presumed that Academy Award voters would forget about *Braveheart* when voting took place later that year. However, when nominations for the Academy Awards were announced in February 1996, *Braveheart* received ten nods, a very impressive achievement. The competition would be a unique one, with *Apollo 13*, the Italian film *Il Postino*, *Sense and Sensibility*, and the smash hit *Babe* all competing for the top prizes. When the awards themselves took place the following month, the industry was surprised again when Gibson, who was not nominated in the Best Actor category, won Best Director, and his saga collected Best Picture of the Year and three technical Oscars. Afterward Gibson, when asked where he was going to stash his Oscars, joked to reporters, "I'm just going to carry them around for a while—for a few days, months maybe, until I figure it out."[78]

Braveheart won five Academy Awards, including Best Director for Gibson.

Several years later, Gibson reflected on that important night at the Academy Awards.

> That directing statue was just such a kick. I was really in the novice camp, and it was invaluable feedback. One doesn't know how you're doing—it's like you're a scientist experimenting, trying to do the best you can, trying to throw it all together and make something cohesive come of it. The award was a great signpost for me to tell me I was traveling in the right direction.

He remains philosophical about his Best Director win. "Many, many people do high caliber work and are never recognized for it."[79] With Oscars, Golden Globes, and a U.S. box-office take of $75 million for *Braveheart*, it had been an extraordinary year for Gibson.

Controversial Comments

But not everyone was happy with—or for—Gibson in the afterglow of his *Braveheart* success. Ever since 1990's comedy caper *Bird on a Wire*, some gay activists had been angry with Gibson. They first took exception with the actor concerning one particular sequence in the film in which his character, a witness on the run from killers, pretends to be a gay hairdresser to avoid capture by the bad guys. They deemed his portrayal a degrading effeminate stereotype.

Then, in 1991 a Spanish publication, *El Pais*, printed an interview with the star in which he allegedly said that he assumed many people might think he was gay since he was an actor. "But I did it. I became an actor despite that. But with this look, who's going to think I am gay?" According to *El Pais*, Gibson continued, "Do I look homosexual? Do I talk like them? Do I move like them?"[80] Gibson was quoted as asking the interviewer. In the aftermath of the interview's publication, he claimed that his words had been taken out of context and misinterpreted, while gossip columnist Liz Smith, along with the gay magazine *The Advocate*, chastised Gibson for his alleged remarks.

Two years later protesters showed up as Gibson was honored on the Hollywood Walk of Fame, just as *The Man Without a Face* was premiering. The activists were upset because Gibson's character in the original novel was a gay man, while in the film there is no real indication of the character's sexuality. In fact, *Entertainment Weekly* later reported, that aspect had been changed before Gibson even signed on to direct and star in the project.

But the last straw was *Braveheart*'s depiction of the violent death of a homosexual character. In one scene of the film, Prince Edward's father, English king Edward I, violently hurls his son's male lover out of a castle window in such a way that seemed to summon a positive reaction from the audience. The Gay and Lesbian Alliance Against Defamation (GLAAD), a watchdog group that monitors media depictions of gay and lesbian people, organized protests in several U.S. cities against what they called the film's depiction of Prince Edward, later the openly gay King Edward II, as a "typical homophobic caricature."[81]

Gibson's defensive response to the allegations of homophobia did not help matters. In July 1995, as the war of words escalated and the topic continually reared its head in interview sessions, *Playboy* magazine quoted the actor as saying, "I'll apologize when hell freezes over."[82]

Making Amends

It was a shock when Gibson agreed to sit down and discuss these concerns with GLAAD's then–entertainment media director, Chastity Bono, and several openly gay filmmakers on the Los Angeles set of 1997's *Conspiracy Theory*. During a luncheon, Gibson and the gay activists discussed GLAAD's problems with him and possible compromises. Although the actor refused to comment about the meeting, his publicist described the seminar as "a nice dialogue between people who have a lot in common,"[83] although Gibson apparently did not explicitly apologize, according to an attendee. There was no discussion of the *El Pais* interview that landed him in hot water in '91, but Gibson did briefly comment on *Braveheart* and his reasons for depicting Edward II as he had, which included fictionalized elements that historians have said were plausible. And although not all were satisfied with Gibson's efforts to make amends, others clearly were. Filmmaker Robert Lee King told

Chastity Bono was the entertainment media director for GLAAD when she met with Gibson to discuss the depiction of a gay character in Braveheart.

Entertainment Weekly, "The impression was created that he was the enemy of our people. Having sat down with him, I don't think that's the case."[84]

Homophobia has not been the only charge leveled at Gibson over the years. A Roman Catholic who is said to be vehemently opposed to both artificial birth control and abortion, he has sometimes been portrayed by feminists as "antiwoman." In an early interview, he spoke out about feminism and certainly did not endear himself to its adherents. "The feminist movement has been in Australia for years, for as long as it's been [in America], I'm sure. And it's just as tired there. One of the most tired things I've ever seen. An altogether unnecessary thing."[85]

Whether people agree with his conservative views or not, Gibson seems to have remained true to his character and the traditional beliefs instilled in him from an early age, even when they have not placed him in the most flattering light. He once told the *Washington Post,* "The term 'politically correct' scares the [expletive] out of me,"[86] displaying the characteristic candidness he has become known for in a town that makes money telling made-up stories.

Chapter 7

Real-Life Roles

WITH THE STEADY growth of Robyn and Mel Gibson's clan have come more family-friendly projects for the star, who is also widely-known as being a devoted husband and father. During the mid-'90s he poured his energy and enthusiasm into several family-themed projects, reflecting his real-life roles and their influence on him. Gibson's other facets include being a loyal friend to many film-industry colleagues and a low-key contributor to many charities.

Husband and Father

The Gibsons are one of the few show-business marriage success stories. Since their wedding day in June 1980, Robyn Gibson has been a loyal and devoted supporter of her husband and his stabilizing force in times of turmoil, and he in turn has lovingly described his feelings for his wife in interview after interview, although he has never been totally at ease speaking about his personal life. One thing he is not shy about declaring is his commitment to his marriage. "I've ruled out the possibility of divorce. I've just ruled it out. I'm not going to do it,"[87] the actor once told an interviewer.

Indeed, although the Gibsons have remained married for more than twenty-one years, like any relationship there have been difficulties for the couple along the way, from his drinking problem to rumors regarding Gibson's alleged carousing with other women in the late '80s. Tabloid newspapers in London, Sydney, and the United States carried such stories. Although Gibson never publicly commented on the rumors of extramarital affairs, a lawsuit was threatened against the tabloids. The suit never materialized; just the same, one Sydney newspaper later ran an apology after printing a story that Gibson had left his family to live with another woman in California. Gibson once explained his admiration for his wife. "She's able to look past my faults and still see something there. . . . Sometimes I find it hard to believe that she can do that."[88] The actor's stunt coordinator, Mic Rodgers, who has worked with him in many movies over the years, disputes the tabloid reports. "I've seen grips and electricians and stuntmen use the business as an excuse when their marriage breaks up," he told *People.* "They say it's because they go on location so much, so naturally they fool around. That's bunk. Mel doesn't play that part of the game."[89]

Who Is Mrs. Mel Gibson?

Robyn Gibson, a dark-haired native Australian, is described as a shy though friendly woman who enjoys the challenges of full-time motherhood to the couple's seven children, including Thomas, who arrived in 1999. She and her husband currently pour much of their energy into their family and volunteer work in Malibu, California, including organizing a youth club and raising money for local schools.

The private couple seems to have done an admirable job of raising their children—out of the public eye. Mel and Robyn Gibson go out of their way to see that their children lead lives in

Look Fast for Gibson

Gibson has made a mini-career out of cameos, or surprise appearances, in films other than his own. Besides the scene as a mechanic (with a beard!) in his friend Steve Bisley's 1980 Australian thriller *Chain Reaction* (also known as *Nuclear Run*), he has popped up in the 1995 film *Casper* (along with Clint Eastwood, Dan Aykroyd, and other big-name celebrities), which was based on the long-running cartoon *Casper, the Friendly Ghost*. In 1997's Billy Crystal–Robin Williams comedy *Fathers' Day*, Gibson surprised audiences as a freaky piercing artist named Scott at a music festival, and in Icon Productions' *Fairy Tale: A True Story* (1997), Gibson plays an important but small role that consists of only two lines of dialogue.

as normal a fashion as possible. When the Gibson children visit or accompany their father to film sets, there is "no parade of nannies," according to *Lethal Weapon 4* executive producer Jim Van Wyck. "They behave and seem to enjoy themselves."[90]

The sense of normalcy for the Gibsons includes the importance of their religion to them. The family attends mass together every Sunday and even spent their vacation in 2000 visiting with Italian monks. Along with such other celebrities as Ricardo Montalban and Juliet Mills, Gibson narrated a portion of the 2001 TV documentary *The Face: Jesus in Art*, demonstrating his interest in theological subjects.

The Gibsons frequently attend one or another child's sports activity, and they enjoy watching films and television together, although most of Gibson's more violent films are off-limits. Parenthood, along with his marriage, has centered him. "Becoming a father helped me grow up a lot," he said in 2000. "You have to do the best job you can do—there's no way out of it. I'm not saying I'm the perfect dad. I'm far from it. But the simple fact of the matter is there are sacrifices to be made, big decisions to be made—any parent knows that."[91]

Gibson rarely, if ever, takes roles that require long periods away from his family and has admitted regretting missing the births of Hannah and Milo while on film sets. He spoke about this recently when reflecting on his choices in film roles. "Years ago I had this offer to go and make *Mountains of the Moon* in Kenya with [director] Bob Rafelson. I liked the story. . . . But if you've got kids, you don't just go off and live in Africa for six months."[92] The family now spends most of its time at two homes in Malibu, California. They also own the aforementioned 800-odd-acre ranch in Australia and a $9.25 million mansion in Greenwich, Connecticut.

An Animated Gibson

In 1995, Gibson performed the voice role of colonist John Smith in the animated Disney film *Pocahontas*, his first G-rated movie. The film, which liberally retold the story of the Powhatan Indian princess, was a hit of *Lethal Weapon 3* proportions, earning just $3 million less than that film ($141.6 million). Several years later a straight-to-video sequel, *Pocahontas II: Journey to a New World,* was produced, but Mel did not participate. Instead, his brother Donal Gibson, now also an actor, took over as the voice of John Smith.

But Mel Gibson did not entirely leave the world of animation or family-friendly shenanigans behind. In September 1999 he guest-starred as himself in the season premiere of *The Simpsons.* The episode, jokingly titled "Beyond Blunderdome," demonstrated Gibson's ability to laugh and poke fun at his movie-icon status as his animated counterpart and Homer Simpson schemed to remake the 1939 Jimmy Stewart classic *Mr. Smith Goes to Washington* as another one of Gibson's ultraviolent action pictures. The show's writers had fun too, naming several cartoon studio executives after members of Gibson's family.

Will any of the Gibson brood be following in their famous father's footsteps with a career in show business? It appears at least two may. Hannah Gibson, the oldest child and only daughter, was a makeup artist on *What Women Want,* giving the film the feel of a family affair. And the actor has mentioned in one interview that his son Louis, born in 1987, has a talent for storytelling and comedy—apparently taking right after his dad.

Ransom

Mel Gibson's facets as father and husband have also memorably translated onscreen. His lone 1996 film also centers around family—this time dealing with every parent's worst nightmare. *Ransom,* director Ron Howard's fast-paced remake of a 1956 picture, reteams Gibson and Rene Russo as the Mullens, a millionaire couple who own an airline and seem to have everything. Their privileged life is shattered, however, when their young son is kidnapped by a band of criminals and held for a hefty ransom. But that's where the story takes an unusual turn. Instead of paying off the kidnappers, Gibson's Tom Mullen turns the tables by placing a bounty on their heads.

Gibson and his wife Robyn own two homes in Malibu, California (pictured).

Originally, Gibson had passed on *Ransom* after reading the initial script, feeling the first draft was not all it could be. He also felt that his character was too perfect, something he has always been careful to avoid. His solution? A little tweaking, with the scriptwriters and the rest of the cast. "We gave the character flaws, made him guilty of bribing union officials, stuff like that. That made his dilemma more painful and real, and I thought, OK, now he's not so squeaky clean."[93]

This was not Gibson's only input regarding *Ransom*. The star also contributed to one of the few action scenes in the film, along with his assistant, Dean Lopata. When Tom Mullen was to initially drop off the ransom, Gibson felt it was too straightforward, too easy. "So we devised another way." Their version has the character dive into a pool, find a locker key, and change cars on the way to the rendezvous. "We just cooked up a scheme between us about how a guy could lose all the tails and radios and microphones. We brought it to Ron [Howard], and he thought it was weird and cool."[94] Audiences reacted warmly to *Ransom*. The thriller, which opened in November 1996, earned $34.2 million its first weekend in release, on the way to an eventual gross of $136.4 million in the United States.

Loyal Friend

Gibson's positive attitude and cooperative nature help to make many of his film shoots happy affairs. As a result, he enjoys many close relationships with Hollywood actors, directors, and other behind-the-scenes folks. This camaraderie is important, since film productions are often delayed or run long, which was the case with *Ransom*. The filmmakers and cast endured some of the worst blizzards in recent New York history during the three-month shoot. As a result of enduring poor weather conditions, many of them came down with colds. The topper was Gibson's emergency appendectomy, performed at Cornell Medical Center in the wee hours of the morning. "That's just like Mel. He loves to one-up ya,"[95] joked friend Howard, whose *Apollo 13* lost at the Academy Awards to Gibson around the same time.

One of his most enduring and rewarding friendships started on the set of a 1994 picture. Gibson first became pals with double Oscar-winner Jodie Foster while making the hit Western/ad-

Jodie Foster and Gibson have remained good friends since costarring in Maverick *in 1994.*

venture/comedy *Maverick*, a big-screen version of the 1957–62 TV series that starred James Garner. Originally Meg Ryan was to play the role of Annabelle Bransford, the supposedly demure frontier wife who crosses paths with Gibson's Bret Maverick on the way to the greatest poker game in the Old West. But Ryan opted out of the project to spend time with her family. Foster, normally known for her dramatic roles, was then offered the part. The actress was eager to perform in a comedy and to share the screen with Gibson, who would be starring in a Western for the first time. "This thing came along on, say, a Thursday afternoon, and I said yes by Friday morning. And I was in costume fittings on Sunday,"[96] Foster has said.

Foster had heard about Gibson's playful pranks on film sets, and she proved to be every bit as willing to goof off while making *Maverick*. One particular scene called for Foster to delicately step out of a stagecoach. Instead, she purposely performed an exaggerated pratfall and was greeted with guffaws from Gibson, Garner (who also played a role in the movie), and the rest of the cast and crew.

Later Gibson would come to his costar's aid when she suffered a real fall at her home. After tripping and hitting her head, Foster received a call from Gibson, who leaped to help his friend. "He came in five minutes with this bag of homeopathic stuff and gave me the Dr. Mel treatment,"[97] a grateful Foster has said.

The two stars continue to maintain their friendship. They are so close that they have nearly two-hour phone conversations, according to Foster. Coincidentally, it was Foster who presented the Best Director Golden Globe award for *Braveheart* to her good pal Gibson in 1996.

Another female colleague with whom Gibson has maintained a close friendship over the years is three-time costar Rene Russo. Gibson even fought to get pal Russo cast as his wife in *Ransom*, after their successful pairing in *Lethal Weapon 3*. "Mel's like the class clown," Russo told one publication. "He's like a hyperactive kid—you're constantly laughing when you're around him."[98] The two friends passed time between filming scenes in *Ransom* by playing Scrabble.

But Gibson's personal relationships are not limited to leading ladies. Danny Glover, Gibson's *Lethal Weapon* partner, now enjoys a strong relationship with his colleague, despite their two very different approaches to acting. Glover remarked about his close friend while filming the most recent *Weapon*, "He has so many incredibly creative ideas and he's always contributing."[99] And during the production of *The Patriot*, Gibson offered guidance to young Australian actor Heath Ledger when Ledger early on expressed some apprehension about his performance.

Devoted Comrade

Over the years Gibson has demonstrated his fierce loyalty to the people he cares about. In late 2000 it was announced that he would direct friend and *Air America* costar Robert Downey Jr. in a Los Angeles stage production of *Hamlet*. Downey had just been released from prison after serving a term on a drug charge and was enjoying a career resurgence with a part on TV's *Ally McBeal*. Unfortunately, the production never came to be, since Downey was arrested again just a few months later.

Gibson's camaraderie with Hollywood's elite extends to his behind-the-scenes colleagues as well. Richard Donner, the director Gibson has worked with most often, has formed a "mutual admiration society" with the star. While Gibson has credited Donner, along with Peter Weir and George Miller, as his inspiration to take on the challenge of directing for the first time, Donner has likewise praised Gibson for his talent and his devotion to his art. "Where do you go for another Mel Gibson?" Donner commented on MSNBC's *Headliners & Legends*. "They don't exist."[100]

Gibson is also known around Hollywood film sets as being just a regular guy—not a pampered movie star who isolates himself from the rest of the cast and crew. While he uses a trailer that serves as a dressing room on the sets of his films, just like any big-name performer, Gibson prefers to visit and hang out with the rest of the production's personnel. While making *The Patriot* in South Carolina, Gibson ate from the buffet spread with everyone else, instead of retreating to his trailer for a private gourmet meal. When his plastic utensil broke, he continued eating with the fragment that was left of it—not most people's idea of typical movie-star behavior.

Charitable Contributor

Most of the time, celebrities' philanthropic endeavors are well-known and publicized in the pages of magazines and newspapers and on TV, from Elizabeth Taylor's work on behalf of AIDS organizations to Sting's rain forest benefits. This is not usually the case with Gibson's charitable works—and he prefers it that way. For instance, it is not widely known that since around 1992 the star has visited sick children at Los Angeles–area hospitals on behalf of the Starlight Children's Foundation, a charity that grants ill youngsters' wishes.

Over the years Gibson has lent his image to America's libraries to promote reading (he is pictured in a poster with George Orwell's *1984*) and to Earthjustice (a legal defense fund to promote

Prior to Robert Downey Jr.'s second arrest, Gibson had planned to direct him in a stage production of Hamlet.

environmental awareness), and he has donated memorabilia from his films for worthy causes. In 2001 friend and fellow actor Liam Neeson asked for Gibson's help with a fundraiser for UNICEF's African organization that works to prevent HIV transmission from mothers to newborns. Along with stars such as Julia Roberts and Sylvester Stallone, Gibson participated, donating his sword from *Braveheart*.

The actor has also made monetary donations to battered women's shelters in areas where he films, such as he did in Chicago during the production of 1999's *Payback* and in Rock Hill, South Carolina, while making *The Patriot*. Although Gibson does not usually comment on his generosity, a writer for *Ladies' Home Journal* was able to extract Gibson's reason for the contributions. "My mother once told me, if you visit someone, it's customary to bring something,"[101] he said.

At Gibson's insistence—along with that of his producing partner, Bruce Davey—the 1992 premiere of *Forever Young* benefited two charities, Los Angeles's Homeless Drop-in Center and Hollywood's Recovery Center, a drug and alcohol abuse rehabilitation center. And for the first time, Gibson spoke about his charitable contributions in relation to his own life. "Alcoholism is something that runs in my family. It's something that is close to me. People do come back from it, and it's a miracle. And I like to be a part of that."[102]

Chapter 8

"Millennium Mel"

AT THE NEW millennium, Gibson mostly takes on roles that cast him as the American "everyman" who triumphs in extraordinary—and occasionally comical—circumstances. These choices challenge his acting ability, diversify his filmography, and ultimately guarantee him a place alongside the all-time, instantly recognizable Hollywood greats who have excelled in several film genres, eagerly promote their projects, and enjoy the respect and admiration of their contemporaries and fans around the world.

Conspiracy Theory

After *Ransom*, the next project for Gibson teamed him with the popular actress Julia Roberts. Interestingly, *Conspiracy Theory* was not the first script they were supposed to bring to the silver screen together. Roberts and Gibson were all set to star in a proposed "Western romantic comedy" titled *Renegades* around 1991, but the project fell apart before production began due to scheduling conflicts, and both stars went on to make other films. So it was with great fanfare that the two were paired for 1997's thriller *Conspiracy Theory*.

In fact, Gibson helped convince Roberts to make the movie instead of taking a vacation. During a negotiation session involving Roberts, Gibson, and the film's producer and director, a brass band was hired to soften the actress up, while Gibson donned a lamp on his head to make her laugh. Finally, she agreed to forgo her time off. But Roberts was not the only one to initially hesitate agreeing to make *Conspiracy Theory*. Working on *Ransom* at the time, Gibson was planning to wait to take on his next project. He eventually wanted to make a new film version of *Fahrenheit 451*, which he would direct, but the project got off to a slow development start. (By 2001, intermittently in development, it was still on hold.) But while Gibson, the first choice for the role, was deciding whether to take the role of conspiracy aficionado Jerry Fletcher, fellow actors such as Jim Carrey and Brad Pitt expressed interest in the part. Eventually Gibson said yes.

Donner directed Gibson in the story of Fletcher, a New York City cabdriver with a penchant for conspiracies. Jerry also happens to have a sweet spot for Roberts's Justice Department lawyer, Alice Sutton. When he stumbles onto intrigue that is much more than just a theory, Jerry and Alice become the targets of a complex murder plot. Along the way, Roberts's character comes to see the cabbie as more than just a paranoid man with a bad handle on reality.

Gibson successfully convinced Julia Roberts to give up her vacation time to film Conspiracy Theory.

Conspiracy Theory enabled Gibson to display many facets of his character's emotional state, from delusional intrigue enthusiast, to hapless victim, to eventual hero. The actor accepted the role of the not-always-stable Jerry out of curiosity and a desire for interesting projects, saying that the film "was risky and prompted the 'Should I do that?' question."[103]

Their were numerous accolades in response, including critic Leonard Maltin calling Gibson's skillful interpretation of Jerry an "edgy performance right on target."[104] The thriller opened in the fall of 1997 and took in $76 million in box-office receipts—a healthy take for the average movie, but somewhat of a financial disappointment to the studio, considering the two major stars (and major paychecks) involved. Gibson has frankly admitted some disappointment of his own with regard to *Theory*, apparently feeling that his and Roberts's star power may have overshadowed the film and its intricate plot. Gibson told one writer, "It's one of those films that might have worked better with people you'd never heard of. It wouldn't have gotten a big weekend, but it would have played."[105]

The Fourth Coming of Riggs and Murtaugh

Although Gibson had declined to make a fourth *Lethal Weapon* for years and even said he would not in published interviews, he again donned Martin Riggs's police badge and gun, and *Lethal Weapon 4*, fleshed out with a cast including Danny Glover, Joe Pesci, Rene Russo, Chris Rock, and Jet Li, opened in July 1998. The third sequel in the series, which by then had made $356 million in this country, finds Murtaugh and Riggs hot on the trail of an Asian crime lord, played by martial arts actor Li. This edition also had Riggs becoming a stable husband and father, much like his partner and quite a change from the 1987 original.

Lethal Weapon 4 also found Gibson performing some of his own stunts, something he does only occasionally. *Lethal Weapon 4*'s stunts included one shot in Las Vegas in which he was dragged on top of a wooden tabletop at fifty mph. "I actually had to work to make it look harder than it was,"[106] he claimed afterward. The sequel also involved a lot of ad-libbing on the part of the stars, Glover later revealed.

Gibson starred in Lethal Weapon 4 *despite stating in earlier interviews that he would not.*

While the film received a generally negative response from critics, there was no keeping the series' fans out of movie houses. The summer blockbuster proved that the partners still had it, with $129.7 million in tickets sold during its run in theaters. Still, Gibson declares that *Lethal Weapon 4* is definitely the final chapter in the series—though he has made that claim before. "You're thinking of seeing if you can make it fly the fourth time. And I think we might have just caught the cliff by our fingernails. Just. I certainly wouldn't try it again."[107]

Hero or Antihero?

If *Lethal Weapon 4* shows Gibson portraying a reformed suicidal cop settling down to family life and mental stability, 1999's *Payback* features him playing the kind of character that Martin Riggs might try bringing to justice. Critics and audiences alike were surprised that Gibson, usually accustomed to largely heroic roles, would play a thief who extracts revenge on seemingly everyone in sight.

Payback's main character, Porter, did have his reasons for the bloodshed (like the Benjamin Martin character in *The Patriot*): His partner had taken his half of the loot from a heist, stolen his wife, and shot and left Porter for dead. What results, after Porter resurfaces, is an ultraviolent fantasy telling the story of a man who just wants his vengeance—and his cut of the loot—a potentially alienating mix for audiences and critics alike.

Although one might not have thought audiences would root for such a protagonist, the film brings to mind such actors as Clint Eastwood, Steve McQueen, and Lee Marvin, who routinely played such unconventional "heroes" to great critical acclaim and popular success. In fact, the movie was essentially a remake of a 1967 Lee Marvin thriller, *Point Blank.*

There was plenty of action onscreen in *Payback*, but some interesting developments also played out behind the scenes of the film as well. Screenwriter Brian Helgeland (*Conspiracy Theory*, *L.A. Confidential*) directed the feature, his first, from his own screenplay. But after *Payback* was completed and test-screened, Gibson, one of the film's producers, initiated rewrites and reshoots when test audiences had trouble rooting for Porter—including a scene in which he physically assaults his unfaithful wife. According to press accounts, Helgeland then ended his involvement in the production, leading some in Hollywood to gossip that the film was "ghost-directed" by Mel Gibson.

The actor subsequently spoke about the uncomfortable parting of ways between him and *Payback*'s director:

> You have to make hard choices and they're hard on other people. Your responsibility [as a producer] is to the production, even if you hurt people in the process. And it always comes down to that. . . . It was tough, and every opportunity was given for the film to be done by [Helgeland]. He didn't seem to want that. Ultimately, the responsibility was to the production. There were hard choices there.[108]

Mad Max Beyond Thunderdome writer Terry Hayes was hired to do some script tweaking upon Helgeland's departure, and about a quarter of the film was then rewritten and refilmed, with Gibson taking on much of the responsibility. The risks involved with and the changes made to *Payback* appeared to pay off for Gibson and everyone involved. Opening in the winter of 1999, the dark thriller sailed to a total of $81.5 million in ticket sales.

Comedy: Romantic and Otherwise

His next two films after 2000's *The Patriot* took Gibson in some new and different directions. Voicing his first feature-length animated role since John Smith in *Pocahontas*, Gibson returned to the recording studio for his second summer 2000 release, *Chicken Run*. The critically acclaimed stop-motion animated film was the first feature-length film from the creators of the popular shorts *Wallace & Gromit* and *The Wrong Trousers*, which the Gibson kids could sometimes be found watching with their father.

Gibson enjoyed the vocal work as Rocky the rooster, and it offered him a liberation of sorts. "You can't be afraid to look like an idiot when you act this stuff out in front of a microphone. Which is no problem," he joked. "I've looked like an idiot for many years now."[109] *Chicken Run*'s plot draws plenty of laughs from the plight of Ginger, a feisty English hen, and her friends as they attempt to escape Mrs. Tweedy's chicken farm, where they are certain to end up as the main ingredients in pot pies. Gibson's Rocky, an all-American bird, looks like the chickens' last hope. But it turns out that Rocky is as scared as the rest of the coop— that is, until the birds band together for their freedom.

Gibson's third, and most successful, film of 2000 found him starring in his first true romantic comedy—and winning raves for his performance. *What Women Want*, released during the holiday season, was also a milestone in his career and in Hollywood history: It became one of the most profitable movies of the year, Gibson's third film to gross over $100 million in the span of just six months, the highest-grossing flick ever directed by a woman (at $182.7 million), and Gibson's most successful film to date.

Remembering *Bird on a Wire*'s not so enthusiastic critical notices, Gibson almost did not star in *What Women Want*. But comedy has long been a passion for the star, and he found the script and his potential costar, Helen Hunt, too good to turn down.

In 2000 Gibson provided the voice of Rocky the rooster (in background) for the stop-motion animated film Chicken Run.

Besides, the mostly female set was a welcome difference for Gibson, whom director Nancy Meyers nicknamed "Millennium Mel" because of his switch from action figure of past films to regular-guy hero of the twenty-first century. "I just preferred the experience of working with women to working with all the guys I usually work with," he said about the *What Women Want* experience. "You don't have to go out in some stinky field and get all sweaty and run up a hill. . . . It was like I was one of the girls."[110]

Well, not exactly. In *What Women Want,* Gibson stars as Nick Marshall, a chauvinistic ad executive who undergoes an electrifying change when he falls into the bathtub with a hair dryer and awakens the next morning with the power to hear what women think. In early scenes in the film, Gibson got to show off a couple of previously hidden talents: In one he performs an elaborate dance with a coatrack and a hat to the Frank Sinatra song "I Won't Dance," and in another he does a flawless impersonation of legendary actor Sean Connery. Displaying characteristic respect for one of acting's elder statesmen, Gibson received permission from Connery to do the impersonation and donated $10,000 to the Scotsman's own education charity for the privilege.

Working hard to perfect his dance number, which included Gibson kicking a hat onto his head, the actor was reminded of his days at the NIDA, which included an "old taskmaster" of a dance instructor. But some things were different too. "I'm not as limber as I was then, for sure, but [I'm better] as far as being relaxed about it. You know, the older you get, the easier it becomes to make a fool of yourself. So I gave less of a hoot about it this time."[111]

What's Next?

Moviegoers can expect Gibson to continue taking risks as an actor—whether or not it translates into box-office gold. The year 2001 saw the release of an independent film in which Gibson had a featured role, *The Million Dollar Hotel.* Based on a story by Bono, the lead singer of U2, *The Million Dollar Hotel* follows Gibson's FBI

Gibson, here at a press conference for the film What Women Want, *wants to give up acting and focus entirely on directing films.*

agent as he investigates a suspicious suicide at the titular flophouse. The film gave testament to Gibson's influence when it opened and closed in limited release in just a few weeks: Gibson had previously made negative remarks about *Hotel*, although he later denied the comments were made anything more than jokingly.

Future projects for Gibson include starring roles in the films *We Were Soldiers Once . . . And Young*, a Vietnam War–era drama that he began filming in 2001, and the supernatural thriller *Signs*. More producing is also on the horizon, including an action-adventure cable TV series and a screen adaptation of the book *Thank You for Smoking* for Icon Productions, which has produced several of Gibson's films, in addition to such others as *Immortal Beloved*, *Leo Tolstoy's Anna Karenina*, and *Bless the Child*.

The star, who considers himself an American-Australian "hybrid," has also said that one day he will take another big risk: give up acting entirely to concentrate on directing films, possibly including the long-delayed *Fahrenheit 451*. "Oh, I know that will happen," Gibson has been quoted. "I just don't know when. Then that'll be it—you won't see me up on the screen anymore."[112]

But in the meantime, Gibson plans on doing what he has been doing—and doing it the best way he knows how. "[The point of doing work is] hard to explain, but you know when you watch an old Humphrey Bogart movie, that feeling you get? It's a Bogart film—just the connotation of quality with the name? I want to be like that. I want to be associated with good work, I'd like people to say, 'It's a Gibson? Then it's gotta be good.'"[113] Whatever Mel Gibson decides to do in the coming years, in front of or behind the camera, one thing is certain: The world will be watching.

Notes

Chapter 1: The $25 Million Man

1. Quoted in Fred Schruers, "The Theory of Revolution," *Entertainment Weekly,* July 14, 2000.
2. Quoted in Michael Fleming, "Mel's Moves," *Movieline,* July 2000, p. 44.
3. Quoted in Fleming, "Mel's Moves," p. 44.
4. Quoted in Schruers, "The Theory of Revolution."
5. Quoted in Fleming, "Mel's Moves," p. 90.
6. Richard Schickel, "A Cheer for Old Glory," *Time,* June 26, 2000, p. 56.
7. Fred Schruers, "The Theory of Revolution."
8. Quoted in Sheryl Berk, "What Mel Wants," *Biography Magazine,* December 2000, p. 126.
9. Quoted in Alex Simon, "The Tao of Mel," *Venice Magazine,* December 2000/January 2001, www.sooma.net/mel/magazinearticles/venicearticle.html.
10. Quoted in Linden Gross, "Mel Gibson: Taking Chances," *Reader's Digest,* August 1998, p. 108.

Chapter 1: Family First

11. Quoted in Berk, "What Mel Wants," p. 54.
12. Quoted in Keith McKay, *Mel Gibson.* Garden City, NY: Dolphin/Doubleday, 1986, p. 8.
13. Quoted in McKay, *Mel Gibson,* p. 8.
14. Quoted in Berk, "What Mel Wants," p. 54.
15. Quoted in David Ragan, *Mel Gibson.* New York: Dell, 1985, p. 78.
16. Quoted in Ragan, *Mel Gibson,* p. 80.
17. Quoted in McKay, *Mel Gibson,* p. 8.

18. Quoted in Berk, "What Mel Wants," p. 55.
19. Quoted in Ragan, *Mel Gibson*, p. 87.
20. Quoted in Ragan, *Mel Gibson*, p. 87.

Chapter 2: Getting Serious About Acting

21. Quoted in Ragan, *Mel Gibson*, p. 89.
22. Quoted in Ragan, *Mel Gibson*, p. 87.
23. Quoted in Ragan, *Mel Gibson*, p. 89.
24. Quoted in Ragan, *Mel Gibson*, p. 91.
25. Quoted in Ragan, *Mel Gibson*, pp. 12–13.
26. Quoted in McKay, *Mel Gibson*, pp. 16.
27. Quoted in Fleming, "Mel's Moves," p. 47.
28. Quoted in Ragan, *Mel Gibson*, p. 98.
29. Quoted in Ragan, *Mel Gibson*, p. 97.
30. Quoted in Ragan, *Mel Gibson*, p. 100.
31. Quoted in Fleming, "Mel's Moves," p. 47.
32. Quoted in Ragan, *Mel Gibson*, p. 105.
33. Quoted in Ragan, *Mel Gibson*, p. 105.

Chapter 3: Serious Actor, Serious Pressure

34. Quoted in Ragan, *Mel Gibson*, p. 20.
35. Quoted in McKay, *Mel Gibson*, p. 38.
36. Quoted in Gross, "Mel Gibson," p. 108.
37. Quoted in McKay, *Mel Gibson*, p. 45.
38. Quoted in Ragan, *Mel Gibson*, pp. 112–113.
39. Quoted in Ragan, *Mel Gibson*, p. 116.
40. Quoted in Fleming, "Mel's Moves," p. 47.
41. Quoted in Ragan, *Mel Gibson*, p. 133.
42. Quoted in McKay, *Mel Gibson*, p. 60.
43. Quoted in McKay, *Mel Gibson*, p. 63.
44. Quoted in McKay, *Mel Gibson*, p. 63.
45. Quoted in McKay, *Mel Gibson*, p. 71.
46. Quoted in Ragan, *Mel Gibson*, p. 149.
47. Quoted in Gross, "Mel Gibson," p. 108.

Chapter 4: Blockbuster!

48. Quoted in Wensley Clarkson, *Mel Gibson: Living Dangerously.*
    New York: Thunder's Mouth Press, 1999, pp. 176–177.
49. Quoted in Ragan, *Mel Gibson*, p. 157.
50. Quoted in McKay, *Mel Gibson*, p. 79.
51. Quoted in Clarkson, *Mel Gibson*, p. 182.

52. Quoted in Melina Gerosa Bellows, "The Word on Mel," *Ladies' Home Journal*, July 2000, p. 97.
53. Quoted in Fleming, "Mel's Moves," p. 90.
54. Quoted in Clarkson, *Mel Gibson*, p. 205.
55. Quoted in Clarkson, *Mel Gibson*, p. 206.
56. Leonard Maltin, *Leonard Maltin's 1996 Movie & Video Guide*. New York: Signet, 1995, p. 747.
57. Quoted in Clarkson, *Mel Gibson*, p. 214.

Chapter 5: Power Player

58. Quoted in Simon, "The Tao of Mel."
59. Quoted in Berk, "What Mel Wants," p. 54.
60. Quoted in Clarkson, *Mel Gibson*, p. 247.
61. Quoted in Fleming, "Mel's Moves," p. 90.
62. Quoted in Berk, "What Mel Wants," p. 57.
63. Quoted in Clarkson, *Mel Gibson*, p. 287.
64. Quoted in Clarkson, *Mel Gibson*, p. 290.
65. Quoted in Gross, "Mel Gibson," p. 108.
66. Quoted in Clarkson, *Mel Gibson*, p. 296.
67. Quoted in Berk, "What Mel Wants," p. 57.

Chapter 6: A New Role

68. Quoted in Berk, "What Mel Wants," p. 57.
69. Quoted in Fleming, "Mel's Moves," p. 90.
70. Quoted in Gross, "Mel Gibson," p. 105.
71. Quoted in Berk, "What Mel Wants," p. 57.
72. Quoted in Clarkson, *Mel Gibson*, p. 320.
73. Maltin, *Leonard Maltin's 1996 Movie & Video Guide*, p. 828.
74. Quoted in Gross, "Mel Gibson," p. 109.
75. Quoted in Fleming, "Mel's Moves," p. 91.
76. Quoted in Simon, "The Tao of Mel."
77. Quoted in Clarkson, *Mel Gibson*, p. 331.
78. Quoted in Clarkson, *Mel Gibson*, p. 332.
79. Quoted in Berk, "What Mel Wants," pp. 57, 124.
80. Quoted in Clarkson, *Mel Gibson*, p. 223.
81. Quoted in Degen Pener, "Gibson's GLAAD Handing," *Entertainment Weekly*, February 21, 1997, www.ew.com/ew/archive/0,1798,1|20021|0|Gibson's%GLAAD%2bHanding,00.html.
82. Quoted in Pener, "Gibson's GLAAD Handing."
83. Quoted in Pener, "Gibson's GLAAD Handing."

84. Quoted in Pener, "Gibson's GLAAD Handing."

85. Quoted in Ragan, *Mel Gibson*, p. 56.

86. Quoted in Berk, "What Mel Wants," p. 57.

Chapter 7: Real-Life Roles

87. Quoted in Gross, "Mel Gibson," p. 110.

88. Quoted in Bellows, "The Word on Mel," p. 97.

89. Quoted in Karen S. Schneider, "Mister Mischief," *People*, July 27, 1998, http://people.aol.com/people/980727/features/cover.html.

90. Quoted in Schneider, "Mister Mischief."

91. Quoted in Berk, "What Mel Wants," p. 57.

92. Quoted in Fleming, "Mel's Moves," p. 90.

93. Quoted in Fleming, "Mel's Moves," p. 90.

94. Quoted in Rebecca Ascher-Walsh, "Ransom Notes," *Entertainment Weekly*, November 8, 1996.

95. Quoted in Berk, "What Mel Wants," p. 54.

96. Quoted in Bruce Fretts, "Funsmoke," *Entertainment Weekly*, May 6, 1994, www.ew.com/ew/archive/0,1798,1|2363|0|Funsmoke,00.html.

97. Quoted in Bellows, "The Word on Mel," p. 144.

98. Quoted in Berk, "What Mel Wants," p. 56.

99. Quoted in Gross, "Mel Gibson," p. 110.

100. Quoted on *Headliners & Legends: Mel Gibson*, MSNBC TV program.

101. Quoted in Bellows, "The Word on Mel," p. 97.

102. Quoted in Clarkson, *Mel Gibson*, p. 316.

Chapter 8: "Millennium Mel"

103. Quoted in Fleming, "Mel's Moves," p. 45.

104. Leonard Maltin, *Leonard Maltin's 2000 Movie & Video Guide*. New York: Signet, 1999, p. 274.

105. Quoted in Fleming, "Mel's Moves," p. 45.

106. Quoted in Schneider, "Mister Mischief."

107. Quoted in Fleming, "Mel's Moves," p. 47.

108. Quoted in Fleming, "Mel's Moves," p. 91.

109. Quoted in Bellows, "The Word on Mel," p. 97.

110. Quoted in Rebecca Ascher-Walsh, "Lady and the Chump," *Entertainment Weekly*, December 8, 2000, p. 34.

111. Quoted in Aimee Agresti, "They Can't Take That away from Mel," *Premiere*, January 2001, p. 38.

112. Quoted in Berk, "What Mel Wants," p. 126.

113. Quoted in Berk, "What Mel Wants," p. 126.

Important Dates in the Life of Mel Gibson

1956

Mel Columcille Gerard Gibson is born in Peekskill, New York, on January 3.

1964

Gibson's father, Hutton, is injured while aboard a train engine; he sues the New York Central Railroad for damages.

1968

Hutton Gibson wins the suit against his former employer; the Gibson family moves to Sydney, Australia.

1974

Gibson enters the National Institute of Dramatic Art in Sydney to study acting; he performs in such plays as *Romeo and Juliet* and *Waiting for Godot* for the next three years.

1977

Gibson appears in his first film, *Summer City;* later that year he graduates from the NIDA.

1978

Gibson meets Robyn Moore; during this time he performs in stage plays and in the Australian television programs *The Sullivans, Punishment,* and *The Hero.*

1979

Gibson appears in the films *Mad Max* and *Tim;* he wins his first acting honors for *Tim:* The Australian Film Institute's Best Actor award and the Best New Talent Award.

1980

Robyn Moore and Mel Gibson are married on June 7.

1981

Daughter Hannah is born; *Gallipoli* is released in the United States; *Mad Max II* is released in Australia (the following year it is released in America as *The Road Warrior*); receives second AFI Best Actor award for *Gallipoli.*

1982

Twin sons Edward and Christian are born during the Australian portion of filming of *The Year of Living Dangerously;* appears onstage as Biff Loman in *Death of a Salesman.*

1983

The Year of Living Dangerously is released.

1984

Gibson appears in three films: *The Bounty, The River,* and *Mrs. Soffel;* arrested on a drunk-driving charge in Toronto in April; son William is born in June.

1985

Tina Turner costars with Gibson in the international hit *Mad Max Beyond Thunderdome.*

1987

Lethal Weapon is released; son Louis is born.

1988

Tequila Sunrise is released.

1989

Gibson stars in the mammoth hit sequel *Lethal Weapon 2.*

1990

Gibson stars in the hits *Bird on a Wire* and *Hamlet* and the flop *Air America;* son Milo is born; mother Anna dies; founds Icon Productions.

1991

Receives the Will Award from Washington, D.C.'s Shakespeare Theatre for his performance in *Hamlet.*

1992

Lethal Weapon 3 and *Forever Young* are released.

1993

Gibson's directorial debut, *The Man Without a Face,* opens to overall positive reviews.

1994

Gibson stars with Jodie Foster and James Garner in the big-screen version of *Maverick.*

1995

The second feature directed by Gibson, *Braveheart,* is released; appears in a cameo in *Casper;* performs the voice role of John Smith in the Disney film *Pocahontas.*

1996

Braveheart wins five Academy Awards, including Best Director and Best Picture; Gibson is awarded the Golden Globe as Best Director for *Braveheart;* stars in the blockbuster *Ransom.*

1997

Julia Roberts costars with Gibson in *Conspiracy Theory;* he appears in cameo role in *Fathers' Day;* has cameo in the Icon Productions film *Fairy Tale: A True Story.*

1998

Lethal Weapon 4 is released.

1999

Payback is released; cameos as the voice of himself on *The Simpsons;* son Thomas is born.

2000

Gibson stars in the hit films *The Patriot, Chicken Run,* and *What Women Want;* becomes the first actor to receive $25 million for a film for *The Patriot;* produces the hit TV movie *The Three Stooges* for ABC.

2001

Wins two People's Choice Awards: Motion Picture Star in a Drama (for *The Patriot*) and Motion Picture Actor; *The Million Dollar Hotel* is released in February; narrates a portion of the TV documentary *The Face: Jesus in Art;* films *We Were Soldiers Once . . . And Young.*

For Further Reading

Aimee Agresti, "They Can't Take That Away from Mel," *Premiere*, January 2001.

Rebecca Ascher-Walsh, "Ransom Notes," *Entertainment Weekly*, November 8, 1996.

Sheryl Berk, "What Mel Wants," *Biography Magazine*, December 2000.

Michael Fleming, "Mel's Moves," *Movieline*, July 2000.

Bruce Fretts, "Funsmoke," *Entertainment Weekly*, May 6, 1994.

Linden Gross, "Mel Gibson: Taking Chances," *Reader's Digest*, August 1998.

Leonard Maltin, *Leonard Maltin's 1996 Movie & Video Guide*. New York: Signet, 1995. This is the granddaddy of all movie and video reference books. Comprehensive, witty, and filled with little-known facts about your favorite movies and stars.

——, *Leonard Maltin's 2000 Movie & Video Guide*. New York: Signet, 1999.

Keith McKay, *Mel Gibson*. Garden City, NY: Dolphin/ Doubleday, 1986. An informative and well-researched book that was published as Gibson's popularity soared in the United States. Focuses mainly on Gibson's films rather than his personal life.

David Ragan, *Mel Gibson*. New York: Dell, 1985. Contains some of the best photos and information on Gibson up to 1985. The family background information is especially well researched and presented. The author apparently had Gibson's cooperation, as well as that of some of his family and friends.

Karen S. Schneider, "Mister Mischief," *People*, July 27, 1998.

Fred Schruers, "The Theory of Revolution," *Entertainment Weekly*, July 14, 2000.

Works Consulted

Rebecca Ascher-Walsh, "Lady and the Chump," *Entertainment Weekly*, December 8, 2000.

Melina Gerosa Bellows, "The Word on Mel," *Ladies' Home Journal*, July 2000.

Wensley Clarkson, *Mel Gibson: Living Dangerously*. New York: Thunder's Mouth Press, 1999. A recent biography of Gibson that contains some interesting, little-known facts but also some speculation. Some rare photos are also included.

"Mel Gibson," MSNBC's *Headliners & Legends*.

Degen Pener, "Gibson's GLAAD Handing," *Entertainment Weekly*, February 21, 1997.

Richard Schickel, "A Cheer for Old Glory," *Time*, June 26, 2000.

Alex Simon, "The Tao of Mel," *Venice Magazine*, December 2000/January 2001.

Index

Academy Awards
  Best Picture award, 11, 73
  Linda Hunt and, 40, 41
Adelaide, Australia, 31
Advocate (magazine), 74
AIDS, 85
Air America (film), 59–60, 84
Alien (film), 38
Ally McBeal (TV show), 84
Amadeus (film), 51
Anna and the King (film), 8
Anna Karenina (film), 95
Apollo 13 (film), 73, 82
Asquith High School, 22–23
Attack Force Z (film), 33
Aunty Entity. *See* Turner, Tina
Australia, 9
  move to, 19–22
Australian Film Institute Awards
  Best Actor award from, 33
  Gallipoli and, 35
Avalon, Phil, 26
Aykroyd, Dan, 78

Babe (film), 73
Bain, Keith, 26
Bates, Alan, 63
Bayside, Maine, 70
Beach, The (film), 8
Bird on a Wire (film), 57, 58
  gay complaints against, 74
Bisley, Steve, 26, 36, 78
Bless the Child (film), 95
Bogart, Humphrey, 18, 95
Bonham Carter, Helena, 63
Bono, 94
Bono, Chastity, 75
Bounty, The (film), 41–46, 48
Brando, Marlon, 44
Bransford, Annabelle, 83
Braveheart (film), 12, 71–74

awards for, 73
box-office take, 74
budget of, 72
challenges of on-scene shoots, 72–73
directing of, 68
reviews of, 73
violence in, 11
wages for, 10, 68
Bryant, Jill, 38
Busey, Gary, 52
Butch Cassidy and the Sundance Kid (film),
  56

Cable Guy, The (film), 8
Camden, Maine, 70
Carolina Panthers cheerleaders, 54
Carpenter, John, 37
Carrey, Jim, 8, 88
Cars That Ate Paris, The (film), 34
Casper (film), 73
Casper, the Friendly Ghost (TV show), 78
Chain Reaction (film), 36, 78
Chamberlain, Richard, 34
Chicken Run (film), 92
Chimes at Midnight (film), 72
Chinatown (film), 53
Christian, Fletcher, 41
Christian Brothers, 21
Clift, Montgomery, 44
Close, Glenn, 62–63
Coast of Terror. See Summer City
Colonel Tavington, 12
Columbia TriStar, 13
Connery, Sean, 60, 93
Conspiracy Theory (film), 75, 87–89, 91
  antics behind the scenes of, 54
  box-office take of, 89
  GLAAD meeting on set of, 75
Coogie Beach, Australia, 47
Cornell Medical Center, 82
Costner, Kevin, 37, 60

Courage Under Fire (film), 8
"Crocodile" Dundee (film), 30
Cruise, Tom, 10
Crystal, Billy, 78
Curtis, Jamie Lee, 54, 66

Davey, Bruce, 86
Davis, Judy, 25, 62
Dean, James, 44
Death of a Salesman (play), 41
De Niro, Robert, 41
Devlin, Dean, 11
DiCaprio, Leonardo, 8
"Dog," 37
Donahue, Phil, 64
Donner, Richard, 70
  concerns about Gibson, 51–52
  friendship with, 84
  sequel to *Lethal Weapon* and, 53
Downey, Robert, Jr., 60, 63, 84
Dunne, Frank, 34

Earthjustice, 85–86
Eastwood, Clint, 78, 91
  advice from, as director, 69–70
  cameo by, 78
El Pais (magazine), 74
Emmerich, Roland, 11, 54
England, 20
Entertainment Weekly (magazine)
  on *The Patriot*, 12
Erin Brockovich (film), 8
Escape from L.A. (film), 37
Escape from New York (film), 37

Face: Jesus in Art, The (TV show), 79
Fahrenheit 451 (film), 88, 95
Fairy Tale: A True Story (film), 78
Fathers' Day (film), 78
Feral Kid, 37
Fletcher, Jerry, 88
Forestville, New South Wales, 33
Forever Young (film), 67
  benefit for, 86
  directing and, 66
  pranks on the set of, 54
Forman, Debbie, 27
Foster, Jodie, 8, 82–83
Fraser, Christopher, 27
French Connection, The (film), 53

Gable, Clark, 41
Gailey, Clement, 33
Gallipoli (film)
  reviews of, 35
  story line of, 34
  success of, 70
Garner, James, 83

Garvey, Tom, 43
Gay and Lesbian Alliance Against
  Defamation (GLAAD), 75
Getz, Leo, 64
Gibson, Ann (sister), 15
Gibson, Anna (mother), 15
  birthplace of, 15
  death of, 63–64
  Ireland and, 20
  on Mel's drunk driving, 47
Gibson, Chris (brother), 15
Gibson, Christian (son), 40
Gibson, Danny (brother), 15
Gibson, Donal (brother), 15, 80
Gibson, Edward (son), 40
Gibson, Hannah (daughter), 23
  as makeup artist, 80
Gibson, Hutton Peter (father)
  birth of, 13
  loss of job, 18
  ties to Australia, 20
  work and, 15–16, 19
Gibson, Kevin (brother) 15, 20
Gibson, Louis (son), 80
Gibson, Mary Bridget (sister), 15
  drama student, 23
  Mel's application to NIDA and, 23
Gibson, Maura (sister), 15
Gibson, Mel Columcille Gerard
  actor training and, 23–25
  alcoholism and, 36, 49–50, 65–66, 86
  animated roles of, 79–80
  awards, 35, 64, 73, 83
  bar fight and, 28–29
  cameo roles of, 78
  charity and, 85–86
  childhood of, 15–22
  conservative views of, 66, 74–76
  death threats on, 39–40
  directing and, 58, 70–71
  emergency appendectomy and, 82
  films of, 9–13
    see also names of individual films
  friendships and, 82–84
  good looks of, 26
  homes of, 50, 79
  labeled "Sexiest Man Alive," 53
  love interests of, 27, 31
  marriage of, 33, 77–78
  "Millennium Mel," 93
  move to Australia, 19–21
  personal life of, 43–44, 59
  possible careers of, 23
  as prankster, 54
  as producer, 91
  religion and, 15, 79
  screen debut of, 26–27
  smoking habit and, 34–35

sports and, 22–23
television and, 27–28
wages and, 8
Gibson, Milo (son), 60
Gibson, Patricia (sister), 15
convent and, 20
Gibson, Robyn (wife), 31, 78
Gibson, Sheila (sister), 15
Gibson, Thomas (son), 78
Gibson, William (son), 47
Ginger, 92
Gladiator (film), 11
Glover, Danny
friendship with, 84
Lethal Weapon and, 50–51
Lethal Weapon 3 and, 64
Lethal Weapon 4 and, 89
Golden Globe award, 83
Best Director, 83
Grazer, Brian, 10

Halloween (film), 54
Hamilton, Guy, 38
Hamlet (film), 10, 60–64, 84
Harvey, Paul, 29
Hawn, Goldie, 57, 58
Hayes, Terry, 91–92
Headliners & Legends (TV show), 84
Helgeland, Brian, 91–92
Henry IV (play), 31, 62
Hero, The (TV show), 27
Hollywood Walk of Fame, 74
Holm, Ian, 63
Holston Valley, Tennessee, 43
Home for the Incurables, 31
Homeless Drop-in Center (Los Angeles), 86
Hopkins, Anthony, 41
Howard, Ron, 10, 80, 81
Hunt, Helen, 92–93
Hunt, Linda, 38, 42

Icon Productions, 66
future project with, 95
Gibson cameo in production by, 78
Hamlet and, 62, 63
Il Postino (film), 73
Immortal Beloved (film), 95
Ireland, 15, 20, 72

Jakarta, Indonesia, 38
Jarratt, John, 26
Jeopardy! (TV show), 19
Jet Li, 89
Jacobi, Derek, 62

Keaton, Diane, 44
Kennedy, Byron, 36

Kensit, Patsy, 55
Kiewa Valley, Australia, 50
King, Robert Lee, 75
Kingsport, Tennessee, 43
Kwan, Billy, 38

L.A. Confidential (film), 91
Last Wave, The (film), 34
Laurie, Piper, 31, 33
Ledger, Heath, 84
Lee, Mark, 35
Lethal Weapon (film), 9–10, 12, 50
Lethal Weapon 2 (film), 54–56
Lethal Weapon 3 (film), 64–65, 83
Lethal Weapon 4 (film), 89–90
Limato, Ed, 61, 65
Loman, Biff, 41
Lopata, Dean, 81
Lord Humungus, 37
Lords of Discipline, The (film), 41
Lovell-Gibson, 62
Lyons, Jeffrey
review of *Lethal Weapon*, 53

Mad Max (film), 28–31, 33, 47
beginning of career in, 9, 12
role in *Gallipoli* and, 34
Mad Max Beyond Thunderdome (film), 48–50, 91
box-office take of, 50
Malibu, California, 78
Maltin, Leonard
on *Lethal Weapon 2*, 55
review of *Conspiracy Theory*, 89
on *The Man Without a Face*, 70
Manila, Philippines, 39
Man Without a Face, The (film), 68–71
Marceau, Sophie, 73
Marion, Francis ("Swamp Fox"), 11
Marshall, Nick, 93
Martin, Benjamin, 11, 91
Marvin, Lee, 91
Maverick (film), 71, 83
Maverick, Bret, 83
McCormack, Catharine, 73
McCullough, Colleen, 31, 32
McGoohan, Patrick, 73
McKussic, Dale, 53
McLeod, Justin, 69
McQueen, Steve, 44, 91
Melbourne Herald (newspaper)
on the Gibsons' arrival in Sydney, 21
Melville, Tim, 31
Meyers, Nancy, 93
Miller, George, 28, 36, 70, 84
Million Dollar Hotel, The (film), 94–95
Mills, Juliet, 79
Montalban, Ricardo, 79

Moore, Demi, 8
Moore, Robyn. *See* Gibson, Robyn
Mountains of the Moon (film), 79
Mount Vision, New York, 17, 44
  property sold, 18
Movie & Video Guide (Maltin), 55, 70
Mr. Joshua, 52
Mr. Smith Goes to Washington (film), 80
Mrs. Soffel (film), 44–46, 48
Mrs. Tweedy, 92
Murphy, Eddie, 10
Murtaugh, Roger, 51
Mutiny on the Bounty (film), 41
Mylott, Alexander, 13
Mylott, Eva, 13

National Institute of Dramatic Art
  (NIDA), 23–26, 64
Neeson, Liam, 86
Newman, Paul, 44
New South Wales, Australia, 13
New York Central Railroad, 15
New York Post (newspaper)
  on *Hamlet*, 63
New York Times (newspaper)
  on *Lethal Weapon 2*, 55–56
No Names, No Pack Drill (play), 33
Nuclear Run. See Chain Reaction

Oedipus Rex (play), 31
Olivier, Laurence, 62
Once Upon a Time in America (film), 41
Oscars. *See* Academy Awards

Papadopoulous, Nick, 26
Pate, Christopher, 31
Pate, Michael, 31
Patriot, The (film), 91
  awards for, 11
  friendships and, 84
  pranks on set of, 54
  story of , 11–12
  success of, 13–14
  wages for, 9
Payback (film), 12, 90
  box-office take of, 92
  charitable donations from, 86
  story line of, 91
Peekskill, New York, 15
People's Choice Awards, 13
Perfect Storm, The (film), 11, 13
Pesci, Joe, 55, 64, 89
Pfeiffer, Michelle, 53
Picnic at Hanging Rock (film), 34
Pitt, Brad, 88
Pittsburgh, Pennsylvania, 45–46
Pocahontas (film), 79–62
Pocahontas II: Journey to a New World

(film), 80
Point Blank (film), 91
Postman, The (film), 37
Private Dancer (album), 48
Punishment (TV show), 27

Rafelson, Bob, 79
Ransom (film), 10, 80–81, 87
Recovery Center (Hollywood), 86
Renegades (film), 87
Rest of Daniel, The. See Forever Young
Riggs, Martin, 12, 50, 90
  suicide attempt of, 52
River, The (film), 43, 58
Road Warrior, The (film), 9
  budget of, 36
  Hollywood attention and, 41, 47
  influence on other movies of, 37
  story of, 37
  success of, 38
Roberts, Julia, 26
  charities and, 86
  Conspiracy Theory and, 87
  highest salary of, 8
  pranks and, 54
Rock, Chris, 89
Rockatansky, "Mad" Max, 28–29
Rock Hill, South Carolina, 86
Rocky, 92
Rodat, Robert, 11
Rodgers, Mic
  on tabloid accounts of Gibson, 78
Romeo and Juliet (play), 26, 62
Running Man, The (film), 50
Rush, Geoffrey, 25
Russell, Kurt, 53, 57, 58
Russo, Rene
  friendship with, 83,
  in *Lethal Weapon 3*, 64
  in *Lethal Weapon 4*, 89
  in *Ransom*, 80
Ryan, Meg, 83
Rydell, Mark, 42–43

Saint Gerard Majella, 15
Saint Leo's College, 21–22
Saladino, Margaret Smith
  on Mel's personality, 18
Salisbury Mills, New York, 18–19
Sammy Award for Best New Talent, 33
Saturday Night Live (TV show), 28
Saving Private Ryan (film), 11
Schickel, Richard
  review of *The Patriot*, 12
Schwarzenegger, Arnold, 50
Scollop, 26
Scotland, 71
Sense and Sensibility (film), 73

Shakespeare Theatre (Washington, D.C.),
  64
Shanahan, Bill, 27
Silver, Joel, 64
Simpsons, The (TV show), 80
Sinatra, Frank, 93
Smith, John, 79, 91
Smith, Liz
  on Gibson and gay community, 74
Smith, Will, 8
Spacek, Sissy, 43
Spottiswoode, Robert, 60
Stahl, Nick, 69
Stallone, Sylvester, 86
Starlight Children's Foundation, 85
State Theatre Company of Australia, 31
Stewart, Jimmy, 80
Sting, 85
Striptease (film), 8
Sukarno, 38
Sullivans, The (TV show), 27
Summer City (film), 26–27, 31
Sutton, Alice, 88
Sydney, Australia, 19–20
Syracuse University, 23

Taylor, Elizabeth, 85
Tequila Sunrise (film), 53–54, 57, 58
Thailand, 59
Thank You for Smoking (book), 95
Thorn Birds, The (McCullough), 31
*Thunderdome. See Mad Max: Beyond
  Thunderdome*
Tim (film), 31
  Gibson's growth in acting and, 32
  story line of, 31–32
Time (magazine), 12
Tolstoy, Leo, 95
Toronto, Canada, 45
Towne, Robert, 53
Turner, Tina, 48

Tuross Head, New South Wales, 13

UNICEF, 86
University of New South Wales, 23
U2, 94

VanWyck, Jim, 79
Venice (magazine)
  on Gibson's desire for variety, 57
Verplanck's Point, New York, 15
Vietnam War, 19, 59, 95

Waiting for Godot (play), 25
Wallace, William, 72
Wallace & Gromit (animated short), 92
Warner Bros., 53, 61, 66
Washington, Denzel, 8
Waterworld (film), 37
Weaver, Sigourney, 26, 38
Weir, Peter, 34
  awards for, 35
  Gallipoli and, 38
  The Year of Living Dangerously and, 70
Welles, Orson, 72
We Were Soldiers Once . . . and Young (film),
  95
What Women Want (film), 80, 92–94
  story line of, 93
Wild Wild West (film), 8
Williams, Robin, 78
William Shakespeare Award for Classical
  Theatre (Will Award), 64
Willis, Bruce, 10
Wood, Elijah, 66
Wrong Trousers, The (animated short), 92

Year of Living Dangerously, The (film),
  40–41, 70
  story line of, 38

Zeffirelli, Franco, 60, 62

Picture Credits

Cover photo: © Theo Kingma/Shooting Star
© AFP/CORBIS, 35, 39
Associated Press AP, 73, 76
Associated Press/News Ltd., 25
© Bettmann/CORBIS, 32, 40
© Rick Doyle/CORBIS, 22
© Mitchell Gerber/CORBIS, 88
Hulton/Archive by Getty Images, 16, 20, 82
© Bob Krist/CORBIS, 44
Photofest, 8, 10, 43, 48, 51, 52, 65, 66, 69, 71, 90
© Reuters NewMedia Inc./CORBIS, 55, 58, 61, 85, 93
© Paul A. Souders/CORBIS, 21
© USA Networks 1998, 30
© Nik Wheeler/CORBIS, 81

About the Author

Jim McAvoy, a Philadelphia native and a member of the Society of Children's Book Writers, has worked in the communications industry for almost a decade. He is also the author of the books *Tom Hanks* (Chelsea House, 1999) and *Aretha Franklin* (Chelsea House, 2001). His favorite Mel Gibson films are 1993's *The Man Without a Face* and the 2000 comedy *What Women Want.*